THE LIFESTYLE DIET

THE LIFESTYLE DIET
Straight from My Heart

DR ROHINI PATIL

HarperCollins *Publishers* India

First published in India by
HarperCollins *Publishers* 2021
A-75, Sector 57, Noida, Uttar Pradesh 201301, India
www.harpercollins.co.in

2 4 6 8 10 9 7 5 3 1

Copyright © Dr Rohini Patil 2021

P-ISBN: 978-93-5422-038-8
E-ISBN: 978-93-5422-046-3

The views and opinions expressed in this book are the author's own
and the facts are as reported by her, and the publishers are not in
any way liable for the same.

Dr Rohini Patil asserts the moral right
to be identified as the author of this work.

All rights reserved. No part of this publication may be reproduced,
stored in a retrieval system, or transmitted, in any form or by any means,
electronic, mechanical, photocopying, recording or otherwise,
without the prior permission of the publishers.

Typeset in 11/15.2 Adobe Garamond at
Manipal Technologies Limited, Manipal

Printed and bound at
Thomson Press (India) Ltd

MIX
Paper
FSC FSC® C010615

This book is produced from independently certified FSC® paper
to ensure responsible forest management.

With Blessings of Shree Rajarajeshwari Devi

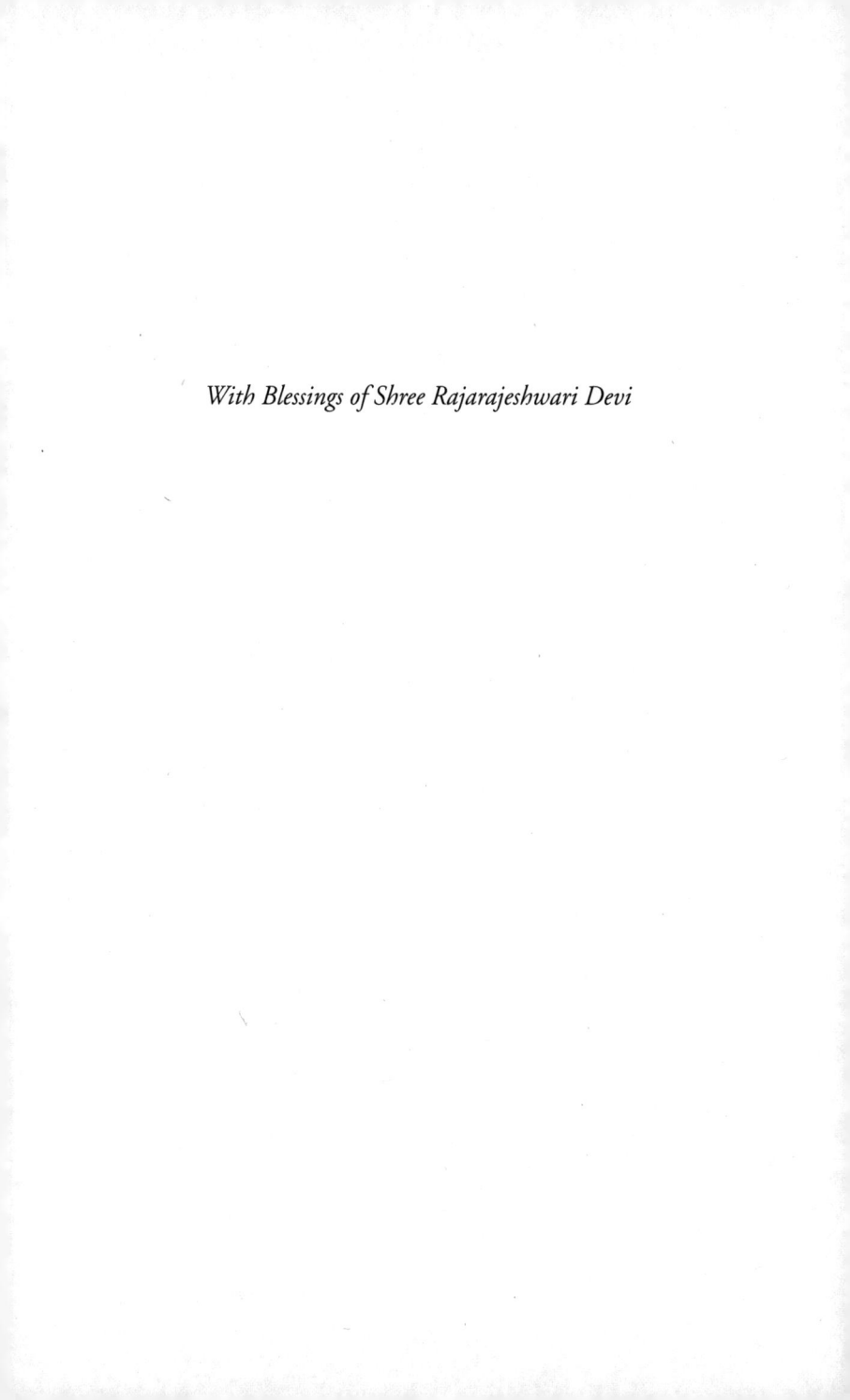

Contents

	A Note of Gratitude	ix
	Preface	xi
1	Getting over the Word 'Diet'!	1
2	Introduction: Combating the Era of Lifestyle Disorders	6
3	Journey towards the Lifestyle Diet	10

SECTION ONE: RULES

4	The Eating Sense—How Do You Develop It?	17
5	Your Gut Is Your Second Brain—Here's Why	21
6	Know the Lifestyle Approach to the Three Magic Meals	27
7	Know How to Fast for Healing	34
8	A Balanced pH Ensures a Balanced Life	42
9	Superfoods for a Super Life	47
10	Reclaiming Our Roots: The Natural Approach to Good Health	88

SECTION TWO: TIPS

11	The Lifestyle Diet	101
12	The Lifestyle Anti-ageing Diet	113
13	The Lifestyle Detox Diet	140
14	The Lifestyle Nutrition Kitchen	144
15	How to Choose Smartly between Carbohydrates, Proteins and Fats	147
16	Food Cravings Are Real—Learn How to Deal with Them	157
17	Lifestyle Habits and You	160

SECTION THREE: RECIPES AND DIET PLANS

18	The Lifestyle Butter Coffee	187
19	The Lifestyle Smoothies	191
20	101 Diet Plans	199
21	The Lifestyle Diary	323
	Bibliography	329
	About the Author	337

A Note of Gratitude

As the popular proverb says, charity begins at home. And, I believe, so does gratitude. Words cannot express enough the love, blessings and support I have received from both my families, and I sincerely believe that this book is an outcome of that support. I would like to thank each and every member of my family for dreaming, aspiring and making it possible for me.

Preface

I PRESENT TO you my latest offering which encompasses several years of practice as a nutritionist and the profound experience that comes with it. My expertise in the fields of diet, nutrition, fitness, mental health and overall lifestyle, and over eight years of addressing various diet and lifestyle disorders have been the inspiration behind writing this book.

Diet and lifestyle are equally important and are often interrelated. There are many common misconceptions around diets and I have encountered several cases of people struggling with short-term diets that led them nowhere. A desire to weave together the different aspects of diet and how it affects the body and mind is something that inspired me to write this book. I wanted to build awareness and share my knowledge and experience with everyone. This book has everything that you will ever need to know about diet and lifestyle and I hope you enjoy reading it as much as I enjoyed putting it together.

As I always say, it's not just a diet but a lifestyle!

1

Getting over the Word 'Diet'!

WHAT IS THE MEANING OF 'DIET'?

DIET IS A pattern of food consumption. Every household, community, country and region has its own predominant diets. In the world of fitness and nutrition, we follow diets or patterns of eating to achieve certain goals. These could be weight loss, weight gain or recovery from diseases such as cancer, PCOD, thyroid, hypertension, diabetes, mental disorders and the like.

So why has the word 'diet' acquired so many different meanings? I hear people say, 'I can never be on diet and that's why I can't lose weight' or 'I can't do a diet and that's why I have PCOD". What they don't realise is that the food that they are eating every day, and the way they are eating it, is itself their current diet. It also indicates that there is something wrong with their current pattern of eating/diet, and that's why they have gained weight or are suffering from a certain disease.

When people ask me whether I am on a diet or if I follow my own diets, I tell them, 'I am always on a diet'. Yes! That's true. I have been on my own diet for over eight years now, and before that, it was my father who put me on a high protein diet since I was a national-level lawn tennis player. Over the last 8–10 years of being on my own diets, I have eaten healthy, taken care of all my nutrient levels and prevented deficiencies, gone out and partied, gone on vacations and tried different cuisines and come back and got on the healthy eating routine again. I have gained weight and tried losing that weight, have enjoyed all my favourite foods and learned to find my balance with them. And today I have found my balance. There is nothing that I deprive my soul of. I eat everything that I love without any guilt or fear of gaining weight. I can say that I am on a lifestyle diet for sure.

And that is exactly what a diet is. It's a pattern of eating, a routine that you follow with your food. This pattern or routine cannot be the same for years together or even months together; it needs to change according to the weather, your health, nutritional deficiencies, health goals, body activity, stress levels, moods and mainly likes and dislikes.

That's why fad diets don't work. That's why, when you follow certain diets, you stop losing weight after a point, remaining stuck. You are a different person altogether, and that's why someone else's diet might not suit you and your body. And that's why we hear people say that diets don't work. It is not the diet itself but the wrong pattern of eating that's not going right with your body. So let's get over the word 'diet' and realise that what you have been eating since childhood and what's eaten traditionally in your house is a diet too. Let's embrace this and make it our lifestyle. You will see more of lifestyle patterns of eating in this book.

Let's talk a little more about diet.

The word diet itself has become extremely popular for the wrong reasons in today's world. Going on a diet is like punishment for people. It is perceived as a process where you starve yourself or deprive yourself of food over a period of time to lose weight and then go back to your old pattern of eating. Let me tell you one thing very honestly: this pattern does not work. Nothing works if you don't pursue it consistently. If you follow a healthy routine for a while and then give it up, you are going to revert to the older version of you.

A diet will not work if you don't enjoy it and make it a part of your lifestyle. It has to be your lifestyle. Your way of living. Something that you truly enjoy. Something that brings out your best version. Something that helps you become a better person. Something that gives you peace of mind. It has to include everything—your good days, bad days, cheat days, festivals, vacations, travel ... each and every aspect of your life. Most importantly, you need to become your own nutritionist.

Yes, I am going to make sure all this is doable and you will know how by the end of this book. And that's precisely why this book is called *The Lifestyle Diet*.

Now let's get into the details of this. Here is a checklist for you to know whether you are following a healthy lifestyle diet:

- ✓ You have good energy levels throughout the day.
- ✓ You are at peace with yourself.
- ✓ The lifestyle diet does not feel like a burden or punishment anymore.
- ✓ You can go out for parties, functions and vacations and enjoy all the food without feeling guilty.
- ✓ You know your body and your relationship with food.
- ✓ You no longer check the weighing scale.
- ✓ Eating healthy is now your favourite thing and you keep going back to it.
- ✓ You are consistently losing weight until you reach your ideal weight.
- ✓ You have perfect glowing skin.
- ✓ You have perfectly thick and shiny hair.
- ✓ It doesn't feel like you're on a diet anymore!
- ✓ You have now figured out your ideal lifestyle.

What is the lifestyle diet and how does it work?

The lifestyle diet is a diet that can be a part of your daily life. It takes care of your physical, mental, emotional and also spiritual health. The best part is that each person's lifestyle diet can be unique. You don't need to follow the same thing that someone else does. You just need to figure out what works for you and what does not. As simple as that. And this book, *The Lifestyle Diet*, will help you figure that out. It will also tell you how to deal with different situations of life in a healthy way. It talks about a healthy diet, healthy foods and most importantly healthy rituals and habits. These lifestyle habits and rituals are going to stay with you forever and make all the difference in maintaining your health in the long run.

So let's begin with adopting a more practical approach. You will find a workbook/diary in the next chapter. Please print ninety copies of the daily checklist and call it your 'lifestyle diary'. This lifestyle diary includes your to-do list for each day. Give yourself ninety days to incorporate these habits and I assure you that this will be the best decision you ever made for yourself.

2

Introduction

Combating the Era of Lifestyle Disorders

We live in a world where multitasking is inevitable and work gets the highest priority, resulting in a world of people with lifestyle disorders. Have you ever noticed this? If not, you will surely come across people with these disorders in the upcoming years. Lifestyle disorders can manifest due to many factors such as stress, obesity, hypertension, diabetes and psychological disorders.

But instead of talking about lifestyle disorders in detail, we will be discussing all those factors that can help prevent them. A healthy lifestyle should be a way of living and not just a temporary fix to nullify the effects of disorders.

We live in a world where not many have the time to keep healthy or stay fit. But once you get into the habit of maintaining a healthy routine, you will be able to perceive and experience the benefits.

For a layman, good health is solely an absence of sickness and ailments. This view is very narrow and one-dimensional. The term 'health' is much more comprehensive. Good health is a state of all-round physical, social, mental and spiritual well-being.

Health and fitness are crucial aspects of a person's lifestyle and have the power to significantly alter their life. Being fit and healthy is not as hard as you think; changing a few simple things will do you a world of good. Small changes can make a big difference.

Fitness is one of the first steps you can take to live a healthy lifestyle. Being active offers benefits beyond an improved physique and a healthy body. You don't have to be a fitness freak to have a healthy body; you just have to partake in a small amount of physical exercise every day. It can be as simple as walking for 40 minutes. Physical fitness is imperative to a healthy life and requires diet, exercise and sleep.

Diet is the kind of food we choose to consume. We must know what to eat, how much to eat and when to eat, as our life depends upon it. Therefore, one should 'eat to live and not live to eat'. You don't have to starve yourself to death to be fit and lose weight. It's more about eating the right foods.

Many people can eat whatever they want and not gain a pound. However, what these people may not realize is that all the food that they are ingesting will surely catch up with them later in life and maybe result in lifestyle disorders or other health problems.

It's important to eat a variety of food items so your body has a healthy balanced diet. Maintaining a healthy diet not only offers your body the energy and nutrition it needs to function but also helps one live longer and lead a better life.

The adage 'A sound mind in a sound body' holds true and you will experience this with some small steps. What works for everybody else may not necessarily work for you. If you want to achieve the optimum level of health and fitness, you should consult a dietician and nutritionist who will tell you, explicitly and precisely, what you should be eating and what you can cut down on.

All you need to do is find a way that works for you. Sustaining a healthy diet is not the only thing to keep in mind; being physically active is equally important. Another thing that many people are not aware of are the mood swings that come from diets that do not include all the nutrients in the right proportion.

Balance is the key! Fad diets and too much or too little exercise can have adverse and long-lasting impact on your body. This is why it is extremely important to have a balance between eating healthy and exercising. However, treating yourself once in a while is not wrong at all. Everything just needs to be done in moderation.

The body should not be taken for granted, because without the body you cannot live life. Be conscious about your life decisions now so that your body does not have to pay for them later. A balanced diet, regular exercise, sound sleep and some meditation are the prerequisites for complete health and fitness, and this in turn is the key to a productive and successful life. Nutrition and fitness are essential for healthy living.

You will not only look and feel good by eating the right things and doing adequate exercise but also lower your chances of getting some life-threatening diseases. It's your decision, at the end of the day, your choice of whether you want a healthy living or not. You should be aware that it is not difficult at all and you can definitely do it. All you need is just a new lifestyle approach to healthy eating and healthy living. Yes, you can do it!

3

Journey towards the Lifestyle Diet

SOCIAL MEDIA AND MENTAL HEALTH

There is so much that I want to talk about in this chapter. It all starts here: healthy body, weight loss, weight gain, good hair, good skin, depression, binge eating, cravings, emotional eating. The chapter covers everything.

We live in a world where we are surrounded by stress all the time. Even for simple activities such as getting to the gym or a yoga class, not only do we have to fight internal battles like procrastination but also face external obstacles—heavy traffic, for example. Many seemingly small things contribute to making our lives constantly stressful—waking up early; reaching work on time; performing our best at work; constantly competing with others all the time. And then there are our virtual lives, our social media engagements. We unknowingly allow all this stress to affect us.

We cannot have a healthy body if our mind is not healthy!

In today's world when we have all the comforts and luxuries, why do we come across so many people with depression, anxiety and many such mental issues? Obesity, hypertension, thyroid, PCOD, diabetes are some of the most common lifestyle disorders today. But the biggest lifestyle crisis is mental disorder or even disruption of mental health.

When we talk about health, mental health is one of the most important aspects of it. Everything starts with our mind—all the diseases, the stress, physical ailments, our intellect, productivity, success, happiness and also our lifestyle. Every person is more miserable today than any of the past generations.

Is it because we have all the information we need available at the click of a button? There are social media platforms where everyone tries to put their best face forward and portray that they are glamorous and happy. Are we constantly looking for validation through the likes, comments and followers we get? And is it that when we don't get that validation, we become miserable?

This generation is not about survival through food, shelter or clothing. It's about the survival of the mind. How are we going to survive mentally? There seems to be a steady increase in the number of suicide cases, and this is not surprising. We constantly see people succeeding in their professions, travelling to beautiful destinations, getting married to the love of their lives and having beautiful kids. They seem to be living their passion, their dream life, achieving the so-called 'life goals'.

Is all that we see on social media true though? If it is, then why are so many people suffering from depression? Are we missing something then? Maybe we are not reading between the lines. Maybe we are trying too hard to showcase our so-called achievements to the world. We are trying so hard that it is draining us. It is distancing us from who we truly are. It is preventing us from finding our true passion. It is keeping us away from connecting to our true selves and living a happy and peaceful life.

First of all, a super happy, successful and happening social media page does not mean that the owner is truly happy and at peace all the time. We do look up to many people on social media. We want to look like them, dress up like them, eat the food they eat, live the life they lead and be as successful as them. And as we chase after this mirage, we disregard the hard work behind that success, the failures that person must have overcome and the pain they might have gone through and still worked relentlessly towards their goals.

No one thinks about these aspects. No one wants to work tirelessly night after night. No one wants to fail so many times. No one wants to go through the pain. Why? Because it's not glamorous? Or because it can't be showcased on social media? Are we scared of being judged? Why are we constantly seeking validation?

Why can't we talk about the painful and difficult phases of our lives openly? Why can't we openly accept that we are going through depression, anxiety or some other mental health issue?

Why can't we happily embrace this aspect of life? I know it sounds really strange but why can't we enjoy the difficult times in our lives?

If we did, the world, and social media, would be such a beautiful place. Things would be more about who we are as individuals and reflect what we have to offer to the world. Suddenly, what we show on social media becomes our real life. Chats on messaging applications have become real conversation. We don't feel happy until we have shared it on social media. We don't feel successful unless people congratulate us on social media. And in all of this constant chaos, where is our life going? Where are we? Are we living a happy, successful and peaceful life?

At the end of the day, it all comes down to this: If we truly want the life of our dreams and want to achieve the so-called life goals, we must focus on a set of things in our life and lifestyle. Not just for a few months, but day in and day out. Try out some of these useful hacks:

1. Unclutter your mind by doing one small thing: do not check your phone 3 hours before sleeping and 3 hours after waking up.
2. Practice deep breathing followed by any form of meditation or just close your eyes and stay still for 20 minutes before sleeping and after waking up.
3. Practice this morning ritual: meditate; list ten things in your life that you are grateful for; do 60 minutes of yoga/exercise/walk.

4. Listen to positive affirmations while driving to work, throughout the day whenever you get the time and while driving back home after work. There are many gratitude affirmations available on YouTube that you can download and listen to offline.
5. Follow this bedtime ritual: write down one good thing that happened to you in the day in your diary (yes, set aside a small, beautiful diary and call it your gratitude diary).

When you start being grateful for every little thing in your life, when you start loving yourself, your outlook towards your life changes and you start moving towards a successful, happy and peaceful life. Your changed outlook helps you handle the challenges better and with a lot of grace. You feel your stress levels (the cortisol and all other stress hormone levels) reduce significantly. You start looking better and eating healthy, your skin begins to glow and you start losing weight.

And from this point, your journey towards a healthy lifestyle begins.

SECTION ONE: RULES

4

The Eating Sense—How Do You Develop It?

THE ART OF EATING

Over the last few years, I have read several books on diet and nutrition, and the art of eating is a topic that occurs in all schools of thought related to diet and nutrition. These are the basics of eating. This chapter tells you how to eat to get all the health benefits of the food that you are putting in your mouth. Without this, even a cucumber could damage your body and a pizza might do it good.

Eating is not just about what you consume. What you eat matters, but how you eat matters a lot more. Eating your food is an art, a discipline, a science, even a framework with several elements that influence how your body and mind process and absorb what you eat. Some people find it incredibly hard to make changes to their diet. Some people love their junk food, while for many others, it is not possible to change their eating habits because of social expectations or religious strictures. And that's okay. It's not the best scenario, but we can work with it.

No food is outright bad or outright good. There are millions of healthy meat-eaters. I know many who consumed alcohol and ate meat every day and yet lived well into their eighties. Much depends on your state of mind. If you are the worrying type or often stressed, even a cucumber can do you harm. 'But I can't help worrying or stressing out', you may say. And that's okay too, as long as you follow healthy eating habits. They will help you feel lighter and healthier. You will sleep better and you will wake up fresh.

The Art of Chewing

Think of eating as a ritual. You sit down, your food is on the table, you mentally prepare yourself to perform the ritual, you start eating and you finish a little while later. Chewing your food well is one of the most important steps in this ritual.

When it comes to the ritual of eating, there are usually three types of people: those who eat quickly and barely chew their food, those who eat at a moderate pace and chew their food well and those who eat very slowly.

If a person eats too fast, their stomach is always strained. The job that should have been done by the hard teeth is left to the soft intestine. Your stomach is designed to bake and not grind; it's an oven, not a blender. The teeth are designed to bite and chew. When your stomach has to digest larger chunks of food, undigested bits remains in it for much longer. Your body has to secrete more enzymes to digest those bits. It makes your internal environment highly acidic. It makes you lethargic, even fatigued. Undigested food creates toxins in your system and is the primary cause of indigestion, migraine and heaviness. Sleep is supposed to freshen and rejuvenate you, but the people who eat very fast tend to wake up tired.

The digestive systems of those who eat very slowly have to work extra hard, much like those of cows, because their food is cold by the time it gets to the stomach. When food is below room temperature, your digestive system has to heat that food to break it down, thus requiring a higher temperature. It is important to note that just because one eats slowly does not mean one is chewing the food well. Many eat slowly because they are doing something else at the same time, such as reading, watching television, talking on the phone or working on the computer.

Chewing your food well is also an important step in mindful eating. Chewing well not only makes it easy for the stomach to digest the food but it also helps it digest the food faster and absorb more nutrients. When you chew food, the salivary enzymes get mixed with the food. The more you chew, the more enzymes get mixed. When enzyme-rich, well-chewed food goes into your belly, your system processes it effortlessly. The acid levels in the body are balanced and the body is free of toxins. Those of you who are forced to follow an unhealthy diet can begin with chewing your food extremely well. Make sure you chew each mouthful at least twenty-eight times.

You can eat your food at the right speed only if you focus on the food while eating. If you engage in any other activity simultaneously, it is not possible to maintain the healthy pace of eating and chew your food properly. Many people are unhealthy because they do not eat their food in the right way. Maintain a steady pace while eating—neither too fast nor too slow—and watch your health improve by the day.

The Art of Mindfulness

Eating is an art. Each one of us practices it differently. If one is cheerful, peaceful and content, the benefits of the foods one eats are much enhanced. That's because such people can digest practically anything. Due to their stable mind, their body stays fit too.

Most people overeat without realising they are eating more than what their body needs. The easiest way to know how much you need to eat is to eat mindfully. Your body will tell you when it has had enough. To absorb the living energy of your food, mindfulness in your eating is essential. Mindfulness requires focusing only on your food while you are eating it: savouring every bite, every morsel. Don't watch television, read or do any work while you are eating. Ideally, you should not be talking to anyone either. All these are distractions. Mindless eating leads one to eat either too quickly or too slowly. If you eat mindfully, you seldom overeat and you benefit most out of your food.

You can test this theory any day. Just go to your favourite restaurant on your own and order a meal. You will find yourself eating less than usual. This is because you are not conversing while eating—you are simply focusing on your meal. Eating mindfully allows even your mind to gain the most out of the food.

5

Your Gut Is Your Second Brain— Here's Why

IT'S ALL ABOUT YOUR GUT FEELING!

YOUR GUT IS your second brain! It could be the real brain too.

Everything that you eat passes from your mouth to your stomach and into your small and large intestines, where, through the process of digestion, the food is broken down by the digestive enzymes. This broken-down food is then transported to the liver by the blood for its conversion into its usable form—sugar into glucose, proteins into amino acids and fats into lipids. These are then circulated throughout the body and utilised by the other organs. So what you put in your mouth influences your brain functions, hormone levels, thoughts and feelings, heart, liver and kidney functions, thyroid and reproductive health. It determines the level of toxins in your bloodstream. This eventually affects the toxicity of the body and its manifestation as a health issue as small as a headache or as serious as cancer.

THE GUT AND THE MIND

Your mood is made in the gut. There is a constant bidirectional communication between the brain and the gastrointestinal (GI) tract. The microbes in the gut communicate with the cognitive and emotional centres in the brain. Seventy per cent of the neurotransmitters such as serotonin are made in the gut and sent to the brain via the vagus nerve. In short, your nutrition determines your mood! Let me explain how this happens. The moment you are done eating junk food such as a pizza or an ice cream, you feel dull and drowsy. Some of you might also feel guilty, knowing that you'll gain weight. This makes you feel very low and negative. A few hours later you feel hungry again and crave some comfort junk food, hoping it will make you feel better. And again after that meal, you feel guilty. You remain stuck in this vicious cycle.

Let's consider another situation: when you eat healthy and exercise regularly, many mood-elevating hormones (endorphins, serotonin) are secreted in your body, mainly in your gut. This makes you feel positive about yourself and everything around you. It also makes you more productive in your day-to-day life and in all the choices that you make. As a result, you keep going back to eating healthy and clean and exercising regularly. This is now a positive cycle that you are in, and it's addictive! Very addictive. Just like eating junk food can become an addiction and make you feel terrible about yourself, eating healthy and staying fit can be a huge addiction that makes you feel amazing about yourself.

Of course, you do have your cheat days—days when you party, go on vacation and eat every dessert possible. But the moment you are home, you settle back into these healthy habits and routines. It's all about striking that balance. If you can succeed in taking care of your physical and mental health, you can succeed at anything in your life.

Everything starts with your gut. Let us look into the science behind how this happens.

Gut flora, gut microbiota or intestinal microbiota is the complex community of microorganisms that live in the digestive tracts of humans and other animals. In humans, the gut microbiota are the largest in number and variety compared to the microbiota in the other areas of the body. The gut flora is formed at one or two years after birth, by which time the intestinal epithelium and the intestinal mucosal barrier that it secretes has co-developed in a way that is tolerant to and even supportive of the gut flora. It also provides a barrier to pathogenic organisms controlling what enters the bloodstream to be transported to all the organs.

The intestinal wall allows water and nutrients to pass through while blocking the harmful substances. When there is an imbalance between the good and bad bacteria in the gut (that is, when there is an increase in the number of bad bacteria and decrease in the number of good bacteria), the gut becomes more permeable to toxins and other harmful substances. This phenomenon is commonly called 'leaky gut'. When the gut leaks and harmful substances enter the bloodstream, they trigger widespread inflammation and a reaction from the immune system.

Most common symptoms of leaky gut syndrome include bloating, food sensitivities, fatigue, digestive issues, skin and hair problems and, in some cases, mental health issues. Chronic leaky gut or gut inflammation can also manifest into conditions such as chronic fatigue, Crohn's disease, irritable bowel disease, thyroid abnormalities, early or premature ageing, cystic acne, mood swings, anxiety, depression, PCOS, migraines, food sensitivities, many types of cancers ... the list goes on.

Let's now discuss what causes leaky gut or gut inflammation.

There are certain foods that are a big no–no when it comes to keeping your gut clean and healthy. They irritate the mucosal lining of the gut by killing the good bacteria and promoting the growth of bad bacteria. I am going to list down the categories of foods that need to be eliminated from your diet to attain a healthy gut and a healthy body. I will also mention the healthy alternatives that you can switch to.

Foods to avoid	Healthy alternatives
Hydrogenated (vegetable oil)	Organic cold-pressed (ghani) groundnut oil/coconut oil/ homemade ghee (cow)
Refined sugar	Organic jaggery/raw manuka honey/fresh green stevia leaves

Foods to avoid	Healthy alternatives
Wheat/maida/any flour or bread containing gluten	Soaked or sprouted brown rice, wheat with fibre (khapali gehu), homemade jowar, bajra, ragi, buckwheat, amaranth, quinoa, any other local variety of millet
Milk and milk products	Almond milk
Antibiotics, analgesics, other medications	Probiotic supplements
Processed/genetically modified foods	Natural and organic foods

Here are some additional notes:

1. You can plant stevia in your house as well and avoid buying it from the store.
2. You can have full-fat curd or yoghurt or buttermilk because they contain good, gut-health-supporting bacteria.
3. Antibiotics, analgesics and other medications kill most of your gut flora. Be extra careful.

Foods and supplements that support gut health:

1. Fermented foods: curds, yoghurt, buttermilk, kefir, kombucha, kimchi, sauerkraut, probiotic supplements. These help in maintaining your gut flora levels.
2. Bone broth or collagen supplements: These help in preventing leaky gut or gut inflammation.

3. L-glutamine supplement: An amino acid that helps your gut heal faster.
4. Zinc and magnesium citrate supplement: These components increase water content in the gut and fasten gut healing.
5. Omega 3 and omega 9: Obtained from flax seeds and avocados; flax seeds are rich in omega 3 fatty acids and avocados are rich in omega 9 fatty acids. They together help in maintaining a healthy ratio of good and bad gut bacteria.
6. Ghee and coconut oil: If you have acne or any gut issue, stop using all other oils and just use ghee and coconut oil. Coconut oil has anti-microbial properties that help in killing the bad bacteria in your gut and increasing the good bacteria.
7. Herbs and spices: Liquorice, turmeric, triphala, ashwagandha, ginger, basil and neem extract
8. Fasting: Regular fasting or intermittent fasting gives a break to your gut and thus helps your gut heal by itself. This is one of the most effective ways of healing your gut.

6

Know the Lifestyle Approach to the Three Magic Meals

THE LIFESTYLE BREAKFAST

As it is rightly said, breakfast is the most important meal of the day. What you eat for breakfast determines your metabolism, energy levels, fat-burning process and productivity throughout the day. It also affects your mindset and thought process. So if you want to be in a good mood throughout the day, have a good breakfast. It is as simple as that!

Also, if you are trying to lose weight, what you eat for breakfast is going to determine the speed of your weight loss.

But what exactly is a healthy breakfast?

The type of breakfast that you should have depends mainly on your health and weight goals. We are always told that the breakfast should be the heaviest meal of the day. Also, you should eat lots of carbohydrates during breakfast, because the amount of carbohydrates you consume at breakfast determines the speed at which your body burns fat. So the lesser carbohydrates you consume, the more fat you will burn throughout the day. Ideally, you should consume most of your carbohydrates for the day during lunch. For breakfast, focus more on proteins, healthy fats, nuts, berries and a small number of complex carbohydrates.

Here is a list of some healthy breakfast options:

1. Homemade idli, dosa, uttapam (homemade batter made by fermenting brown rice and urad dal in equal quantities) with coconut chutney
2. Homemade ragi idli, dosa and uttapam with coconut chutney
3. Indian paratha or thalipith with pudina chutney (paratha or thalipith flour ingredients given separately below)
4. Two whole eggs bhurji (cooked in ghee) + half avocado (fat-burning breakfast)
5. Homemade yoghurt or curd with a banana, berries, ten almonds, ten walnuts, one tablespoon pumpkin seeds and one tablespoon flax seeds (fat-burning breakfast bowl)

6. Breakfast smoothie that can include spinach, curd, banana, apple, five almonds, five walnuts, five cashews, one tablespoon pumpkin seeds, one tablespoon chia seeds
7. Brown rice porridge, ragi porridge or bajra porridge

There is some confusion that I want to clear about white rice and brown rice. When you compare both brown and white rice, you realise that as compared to white rice, brown rice is richer in fibre, B-complex vitamins and other micronutrients. The problem is its digestibility, because of which many nutritionists recommend white rice over brown rice. The reason why brown rice is difficult to digest is phytic acid, a constituent that is difficult to digest and interferes with the absorption of other nutrients in the gut. Also responsible for germination, this is a natural compound present in brown rice and many other lentils. When seeds are given the right environmental conditions and enough water, phytic acid is released and the process of germination begins. Similarly, when we consume brown rice or any other lentils (moong, matki, masoor, peas, rajma and the like), they should either be soaked overnight (for a minimum of 6 hours) or they should be sprouted. I would recommend the sprouted ones over the soaked. They get cooked faster. They are very easy to digest. And they have multiple health benefits. I am going to list some of them down here.

Health benefits of sprouting or soaking brown rice, wheat and all the lentils and beans:

1. Sprouts consist of a remarkably high amount of living enzymes. These further enhance your metabolism and

improve chemical reactions within the body, specifically when it comes to digestion. Enzymes are very effective in breaking down the food and enhancing the absorption of nutrients by the digestive tract. Sprouts also contain huge amounts of dietary fibre that regulates digestion. This helps in the overall improvement of your digestive health and prevents chronic or acute constipation.
2. People suffering from gluten intolerance can consume sprouted wheat or sourdough bread. They are digested well and do not cause any gut irritation or inflammation.
3. They are super filling and avert any other craving by satisfying your hunger. Thus, they help in weight loss.
4. Sprouts are one of the best sources of digestible protein for vegetarians and vegans.

So, if you ever have to choose between white rice and brown rice, choose soaked or sprouted brown rice. In case soaked or sprouted brown rice is not available, go for white rice.

LET'S TALK ABOUT THE LIFESTYLE LUNCH

Honestly, lunch is my favourite meal of the day. This is the time I enjoy all my carbohydrates without any guilt. It is the time I make sure I consume a wholesome meal with almost everything in it. I know how hard it can get for some people to get on a different or a new pattern of eating, and they end up craving the normal Indian roti–sabzi. So this is the time when you can have a proper Indian meal or consume all your favourite carbohydrates or even enjoy your cheat meal (if you plan on cheating).

Some of the best lunch options are listed below:

1. 1–2 millet rotis (ragi, jowar, bajra, quinoa or any other) + 1 bowl sabzi + 1 bowl dal + 1 bowl homemade raita or dahi
2. Idli + sambar + coconut chutney
3. Sprouted brown rice + rajma/moong/egg/chicken/fish curry + 1 glass solkadi (coconut-based)

It is always good to keep your lunch simple and basic so that you can try more options and variations for breakfast and dinner.

Now let's talk about the meal that plays a major role in your health and weight-loss journey.

THE LIFESTYLE DINNER

If you want to lose weight, stay fit or maintain yourself, all you need to do is fix your dinner timings. The world we live in eats at 9:00 p.m. and sleeps at 1:00 a.m. and again eats breakfast at 8:00 a.m. First of all, you need to keep a gap of 4–6 hours between your last meal and sleep time. Before you sleep, the process of digestion needs to be over and your body, especially your digestive system, should get enough rest and recovery for proper functioning. If you fall asleep with undigested food in your gut, you will not only gain weight but also end up with multiple digestive and other diseases. To simplify it further, you should maintain a gap of 12–14 hours between your last meal of the previous day and the first meal of the following. Now according to your convenience, you can manage your dinner timings. Of course, it is hard initially and you get those hunger pangs at your usual dinner time, but remember this is only because of a habit. The human body is a slave of its habits. So just give yourself a week to adjust to the new dinner timings and I promise this will be one of the best lifestyle changes you have ever made!

Now, what does an ideal dinner look like?

Well, it varies from person to person and changes according to your goals. Dinner is one meal that is going to decide everything for you: your weight, your overall health, your body type, the speed of your weight loss or inch loss, your productivity the next day and also the quality of your sleep.

Here are some of the best food combinations for dinner:

1. Soups + salads + good protein
2. Protein + good fats
3. Protein + good fats + starchy root tubers such as sweet potato
4. Dal rice and ghee
5. Dal khichadi and ghee
6. Quinoa or millet upma with ghee
7. Sabzi and dal with no additional complex carbohydrate

(Please refer to the chapter 'How to Choose Smartly Between Carbohydrates, Proteins and Fats' to know what food options belong to each category.)

There are so many different ways of fixing a healthy dinner for yourself. But above all, when it comes to dinner, your timing plays a major role and makes all the difference.

7

Know How to Fast for Healing

THE PRACTISE OF fasting has been part of our country's culture for over thousands of years now. There is a lot of literature on fasting in Ayurveda and many ancient medical texts. In current times, trends such as intermittent fasting and one-meal-a-day (OMAD) diet offer a completely fresh perspective on the age-old fasting ritual.

WHAT IS FASTING?

Fasting is abstinence from eating—it's that simple. All you have to do is not eat when you are fasting. Sounds easy right? But at the same time, it is one of the most complex and most studied concepts in the field of diet and nutrition. So let's learn all about fasting and how exactly we can use it to enhance our lifestyle in all the aspects (physically, mentally and spiritually).

The main reason why fasting is one of the most popular and vastly followed practices in the world is its powerful effect on longevity and how it prepares the body to heal itself from within. This chapter will delve deeper into the mechanisms and benefits of autophagy and simple ways to adopt it as a lifestyle.

What is autophagy?

Autophagy or autophagocytosis is a technical word used in science and translates from an ancient Greek word 'autophagy' which means self-digestion or 'eating of the self'. Autophagy is a metabolic process during which the cells disassemble and remove their dysfunctional components. Your body is basically recycling debris from the cells and putting out the trash.

In earlier studies, it was thought that autophagy was a hormonal response to starvation, but recent research has shown that autophagy has several other roles in biology. The benefits of autophagy include reduced inflammation, improved immunity, prevention of stress and ageing, suppression of cancerous tumour cells, elimination of pathogens, cellular cleansing, weight loss, improved energy levels, improved focus and improved performance and productivity. It is one of the best ways by which our body expels cellular junk to promote new cell growth.

How does autophagy work?

Autophagy is a biological process in which the key players are tiny cells called lysosomes. These contain enzymes needed to digest and break down parts of the cell that no longer function properly. Cellular cleansing is essential because junk lying around in our cells causes them to deteriorate and become less efficient. When our cells are not working properly, our body becomes more susceptible to degeneration. Autophagy makes our body more efficient, stops cancerous growth and prevents metabolic dysfunction conditions such as diabetes and obesity.

Where do you start intermittent fasting?

This is quite simple. You can begin whenever you feel you need to pay attention to your health. When you want to improve your performance and productivity. When you want to stop popping all those pills to control lifestyle disorders. When you feel you want to look young and age as gracefully as possible.

What are the different ways in which you can practise intermittent fasting?

1. 12 hours of fasting: Anyone can do this. It is very easy and quite a few of you must be doing it even now without realising it. You have your dinner at 8:00 p.m. and your next meal at 8:00 a.m. the next morning. Or whenever you have your last meal of the day, have the next one after 12 hours. This is the best way to get on with the journey if you are used to munching frequently. How often can you do this? Ideally, this should be your daily lifestyle. You should ensure a minimum interval of 12 hours between your dinner and breakfast. So you can do it every single day of your life.

2. 16:8 intermittent fasting: Here, 16 and 8 indicate the fasting and eating windows. The 'fasting window' is the period when you cannot consume any foods that increase blood sugar and release insulin, since this will break the fast. The 'eating window' is the period when you can eat, i.e. feed and nourish your body. In 16:8 type of fasting, you will fast for 16 hours and eat in the remaining 8 hour window. This is the basic variety of intermittent fasting that you must adopt to enjoy most of its health benefits. The 16:8 type of intermittent fasting can become your new lifestyle.

   Example 1: If you have your last meal of the day at 8:00 p.m., then have your first meal at noon the next day. You will be skipping breakfast but you can still fit in three meals in your 8 hour eating window between 12 p.m. and 8 p.m.

   Example 2: If you are a morning person and have to have to eat in the morning, you can have your dinner at 6:00 p.m. and breakfast (where you will be breaking your fast as the word suggests) at 10:00 a.m. the next morning. This type of intermittent fasting can also be a part of your weekdays' lifestyle. You can easily do it for six days a week and enjoy one day of eating whenever you want.

3. 20:4 intermittent fasting: This type of fasting should only be done once or twice a week. For the rest of the week, you should fast for either 16 or 18 hours. A 20-hour fast falls under the long fasts category, which gives you the best healing and anti-ageing benefits of fasting. You can break

this fast with a butter coffee or a protein shake and move on to your one healthy meal for the day!

Foods to have in the fasting window	Foods to break your fast
Lemon water	Butter coffee/ghee coffee/coconut coffee
Black coffee (no milk, no sugar)	Almonds, walnuts
Herbal teas, kadhas (no sugar/jaggery/honey)	Plant-based protein shake, high-protein low-glycaemic smoothie
Green tea	Avocados
1 tsp raw unfiltered apple cider vinegar (ACV) in 500 ml water	Eggs, fish (grilled)
Lukewarm water throughout the day	Moong or besan chillas cooked in ghee

Practices that will help you get maximum benefits out of intermittent fasting:

1. Exercise: Exercise is one of the most effective ways to boost autophagy in the body. Exercise is a body stressor and the body induces autophagy so that your cells can recover from the stress. All it takes is 30 minutes of aerobic exercise to activate autophagy in the brain.
2. Low-carbohydrate diet: A low-carbohydrate diet helps you get most of your calories from healthy fats and proteins. As a result, your body and brain function way better and smoother than they do on a high-carbohydrate diet.

3. Deep sleep: Circadian rhythm, melatonin and deep sleep are very important for your body's healing and recovery. So make sure you sleep well for at least 7–8 hours a day.

Foods that help you heal from within and also enhance the benefits of fasting:

- Black coffee: Drinking coffee is also a way to induce autophagy in the body. The polyphenols in coffee have good antioxidant effects on the body. However, coffee can disrupt sleep, so make sure you have your last cup of coffee before 4:00 p.m.
- Green tea: Green tea is known to have anti-inflammatory, anti-ageing and neuroprotective effects on the body. Have at least 2–3 cups of green tea throughout the day.
- Coconut oil: Since coconut oil is a rich source of medium chain triglycerides (MCTs), it helps you sustain much better through your fasting hours and keeps your blood sugar levels stable.
- Herbs and spices such as ginger, ginseng, turmeric, reishi mushroom, cinnamon, maca and asafoetida. All of them help in healing your body from within, so make sure you include them in your foods during the 'eating window'.

> **Did you know?**
> Calorie restriction activates anti-ageing genes called sirtuins, which help reverse certain epigenetic changes that can cause premature ageing.

Please find all the intermittent fasting diet plans in the last chapter. There are lots of surprises waiting for you there!

CASE STUDY 1	
Client profile	• Age: 42 years • Weight: 61 kg • Height: 5 ft. 2 in. • BMI: 29 (borderline obesity)
Medical complications	• Poly-cystic ovarian disease (detected through ultrasound) • Weight-gain issues
Other complaints	• Hairfall • Acne • Unwanted hair growth • Mood swings • Low self esteem • Disturbed sleep (5–6 hours per night)
Existing diet and exercise routine	• Habit of binge-eating sweets • Walk once per week
Diet changes recommended	• Foods that balance sugar levels without adding calories • Intermittent fasting to balance hormones • Special butter coffee • Lunch: green vegetables, salad, brown rice • Collagen supplement to tackle skin and hair issues • Refer to diet plan nos 61 and 63

CASE STUDY 1	
Exercise routine recommended	• Initially, only light exercises • Yoga (3 times a week) • Walk (5 times a week) • Light cardio (different exercises every fortnight)
Other recommendations	• Meditation
Improvement in condition	• Weight loss of 3.5 kg • Acne under control • Reduction in number and size of follicles • After two months, complete control of PCOS and acne issue • Further 3 kg decrease in weight to 54.5 kg • Reduction in BMI to 24

8
A Balanced pH Ensures a Balanced Life

---·---

THE ALKALINITY OF your food plays a major role in slowing down the ageing process. It also significantly impacts your gut health. When your diet is highly alkaline, it ensures that the pH of your gut is on the alkaline side. The alkalinity of your gut is necessary for all the good bacterial flora, and it also kills the bad bacteria or any other toxics in your gut and your bloodstream.

Here are the health benefits of a highly alkaline diet:

1. It protects bone density and muscle mass.
Your mineral intake plays an important role in the development and maintenance of bone structures. Research shows that the

more alkalising fruits and vegetables someone eats, the better protection they get from decreased bone strength and muscle wasting as they age.

An alkaline diet can help balance ratios of minerals that are important for building bones and maintaining lean muscle mass, including calcium, magnesium and phosphate. Alkaline diets also help improve the production of growth hormones and vitamin D absorption, which further protects bones, in addition to mitigating several other chronic diseases.

2. It lowers the risk of hypertension and stroke.
One of the anti-ageing effects of an alkaline diet is that it decreases inflammation and enhances growth-hormone production. This has been shown to improve cardiovascular health and protect against common problems such as high cholesterol, hypertension (high blood pressure), kidney stones, stroke and even memory loss.

3. It reduces chronic pain and inflammation.
Studies have found a connection between an alkaline diet and reduced chronic-pain levels. Chronic acidosis has been found to contribute to chronic back pain, headaches, muscle spasms, menstrual symptoms, inflammation and joint pain.

4. It boosts vitamin absorption and prevents magnesium deficiency.
An increase in magnesium is required for the function of hundreds of enzyme systems and bodily processes. Many people

have magnesium deficiencies and therefore suffer from heart complications, muscle pains, headaches, sleep trouble and anxiety. Magnesium is also required to activate vitamin D and prevent vitamin D deficiency, which is important for overall immunity and endocrine functioning.

5. It helps improve immune function and offers cancer protection.

When cells lack enough minerals to properly dispose of waste or oxygenate the body fully, the whole body suffers. Vitamin absorption is compromised by mineral loss, while toxins and pathogens accumulate in the body and weaken the immune system.

Research published in the *British Journal of Radiology* showed that cancerous cell death (apoptosis) was more likely to occur in an alkaline body. Cancer prevention is believed to be associated with an alkaline shift in pH due to alteration in electric charges and the release of basic protein components. Alkalinity can help decrease inflammation and the risk for diseases such as cancer. Plus, an alkaline diet has been shown to be more beneficial for some chemotherapeutic agents that require a higher pH to be effective.

6. It can help you maintain a healthy weight.

Limiting the consumption of acidic foods and eating more alkaline foods can prevent obesity by decreasing leptin levels and inflammation, which affect your hunger and fat-burning abilities. Since alkaline foods are anti-inflammatory foods, consuming them gives your body a chance to achieve normal leptin levels and feel satisfied upon eating the number of calories you really need.

An alkaline pH level helps you effectively fight any bacterial or viral infection because alkaline pH supports and boosts your immune cells, giving you stronger immunity.

Let us look at alkaline foods from different food categories.

Vegetable sources		
• All greens	• Celery	• Bitter Gourd
• Carrots	• Spinach	• Cabbage
• Beetroot	• Bell peppers	• Pumpkin
• French beans	• Avocado	• Broccoli
• Fermented vegetables (Chinese pickles)	• Parsley	• Asparagus
	• Kale	
	• Fresh coriander	
• Sweet Potato	• Cauliflower	
• Squashes	• Radish	
Protein sources		
• Millets (all bhakris)	• Green peas	• Pumpkin seeds
	• Tofu	• Chia seeds
• Quinoa	• Yoghurt	
• Buckwheat	• Almonds	
• Sunflower seeds	• Flax seeds	
Fruit sources		
• Berries	• Kiwi	• Plum
• Banana	• Muskmelon	
• Raisins	• Passion fruit	

Spices and seasoning sources		
• Cinnamon	• Thyme	• Sea salt
• Curry leaves	• Cumin	• All herbs
• Ginger	• Garlic	

Other alkaline foods and oils sources	
• Lime water	• Coconut oil
• Ghee	• Sesame oil

Being on an alkaline diet does not mean that you completely change your diet and follow an alkaline diet for a short time span; it simply means that you should incorporate maximum alkaline foods in your existing daily diet. This will give you the maximum benefits from alkaline foods.

9

Superfoods for a Super Life

S UPERFOODS. GOSH! THIS word is completely overused these days. Weight-loss superfoods, skin superfoods, hair superfoods… and the list goes on. So, what are superfoods? Though they are marketed as such, they are not some magic potion that will immediately resolve all your health concerns. Superfoods are foods that we include in our diet to improve our overall health and wellness.

Here, it is important to know that superfoods can be 5 to 10 per cent of your total diet, but they work best only when they are blended with a wholesome diet and foods that help you heal.

LET'S TAKE A LOOK AT SOME SUPERFOODS

Raw Unfiltered Apple Cider Vinegar

Despite ACV recently becoming popular, its wide-ranging benefits have been well-known for over hundreds of years. It's been found to control blood sugar, promote weight loss, and even heal acne and blemishes.

ACV is made from apple cider that has been fermented to form healthy probiotics and enzymes, giving it considerably less sugar and thereby reducing calories in comparison with apple cider or apple juice. One to two tablespoons of ACV are good enough to give you its health benefits, and each tablespoon gives you around three to five calories and minimal sugar.

With more than twenty latent uses and multitude health benefits, this is a very important item in your medicine cabinet.

1. Regulates blood sugar levels

Research and studies have proven the ability of ACV to help maintain normal blood sugars. Studies have found that ACV consumption actually helped decrease blood sugar levels by an average of 31 per cent after eating white bread.

ACV can also increase the sensitivity to insulin, a hormone responsible for transporting sugar from the blood to the tissues where it can be used as fuel. Maintaining a high level of insulin in the body can cause insulin resistance, which reduces its effectiveness and leads to high blood sugar and diabetes. A study in *Diabetes Care* showed that vinegar ingestion helped significantly improve insulin sensitivity up to 34 per cent in those with either type 2 diabetes or insulin resistance.

To keep blood sugar levels stable, dilute one to two tablespoons of ACV in one glass of water and consume before meals. Additionally, be sure to moderate carbohydrate intake, increase your consumption of fibre and protein foods and get in plenty of regular physical activity to drop blood sugar levels even more.

2. Enhances weight loss
ACV has been in the spotlight lately with fitness enthusiasts and natural health experts alike endorsing an ACV diet to help lose unwanted pounds quickly. But is ACV good for weight loss?

You can find much research confirming the benefits of ACV for weight loss. In one study, consuming just two tablespoons per day of ACV over twelve weeks resulted in nearly four pounds of weight loss with no other modifications to diet or lifestyle.

Studies show that ACV may also increase satiety. Nevertheless, using ACV as a quick fix for weight loss is not right. Just drinking it alone will not help either, and the amount of ACV weight loss will be minimal. You need to combine this with a healthy diet and active lifestyle to obtain sustainable results.

3. Lowers cholesterol
Cholesterol is a fat that builds in and blocks arteries, causing them to narrow and harden. High blood cholesterol puts unnecessary strain on the heart, forcing it to work harder to

push blood throughout the body. ACV can keep the heart healthy by keeping cholesterol levels low.

Along with a tablespoon or two of ACV in your diet each day, other ways to lower cholesterol include curtailing your intake of sugar and refined carbohydrates, including a good variety of healthy fats in your diet and eating a few servings of fish per week.

Coconut Oil (Cold-Pressed Coconut Oil)

You can find more than 1,500 studies that have already proven coconut oil to be one of the healthiest foods on the planet. There are several benefits of coconut oil that have still not been discovered and innumerable uses that are beyond what people know. Coconut oil is made from copra or dried coconut flesh and is in actual terms a true superfood.

Research has finally uncovered the secrets to this amazing superfood: namely, healthy fats called medium-chain fatty acids (MCFAs). These unique fats include:

- Caprylic acid
- Lauric acid
- Capric acid

Around 62 per cent of the oils in coconut are made up of these three healthy fatty acids, and 91 per cent of the fat in coconut oil is healthy saturated fat. This fat composition makes it one of the most beneficial fats on the planet, as the USDA nutrient database shows.

Most of the fats we consume take longer to digest, but MCFAs found in coconut oil provide the perfect source of energy because they only have to go through a three-step process to be turned into fuel as opposed to other fats that have to go through a twenty-six-step process!

Unlike long-chain fatty acids found in plant-based oils, MCFAs are:

- Easy to digest
- Not readily stored as fat
- Antimicrobial and antifungal
- Small in size, allowing easier cell permeability for immediate energy
- Processed by the liver, which means that they're immediately converted into energy instead of being stored as fat.

All of this explains why this oil made from copra makes for a true superfood and how its benefits are plentiful and amazing.

Here are some of the benefits of coconut oil:

1. Proven natural treatment for Alzheimer's disease

The digestion of MCFAs by the liver creates ketones that are readily accessible by the brain for energy. Ketones supply energy to the brain without needing insulin to process glucose into energy.

Recent research has shown that the brain creates its insulin to process glucose and power brain cells. As the brain of an Alzheimer's patient loses the ability to create its insulin, the ketones from coconut oil could create an alternate source of energy to help repair brain function.

2. Prevents heart disease and high blood pressure
Coconut oil is high in natural saturated fats. Saturated fats not only increase the healthy cholesterol (known as HDL cholesterol) in your body but also help convert the LDL 'bad' cholesterol into good cholesterols.

Increasing the HDL in the body helps promote heart health and lower the risk of heart disease. Coconut oil also benefits the heart by lowering high triglycerides.

3. Treats UTI and kidney infection, and protects the liver
Coconut oil has been known to clear up and heal urinary tract infections (UTIs) and kidney infections. The MCFAs in the oil work as a natural antibiotic by disrupting the lipid coating on bacteria and killing them. Research also shows that coconut oil directly protects the liver from damage.

Coconut water also helps hydrate and support the healing process. Doctors have even injected patients with coconut water to clear up kidney stones.

4. Reduces inflammation and arthritis
In a study in India, the high levels of antioxidants present in virgin coconut oil (VCO) reduced inflammation and effectively treated arthritis.

In another recent study, coconut oil that was harvested with only medium heat was found to suppress inflammatory cells. It worked as both an analgesic and as an anti-inflammatory agent.

5. Cancer prevention and treatment

Coconut oil has two qualities that help it fight cancer: the first are the ketones produced in digesting it. Tumour cells are not able to access the energy in ketones and are glucose dependent. It's believed that a ketogenic diet could be a possible component of helping cancer patients recover.

Two, as the MCFAs digest the lipid walls of bacteria, they also can kill the helicobacter pylori bacteria that are known to increase the risk of stomach cancer. Even in studies where cancer is chemically induced, the consumption of coconut oil prevents cancer from developing.

6. Immune system boost (antibacterial, antifungal and antiviral)

Many diseases today are caused by the overgrowth of bad bacteria, fungi, viruses and parasites in the body. Coconut oil contains lauric acid (monolaurin), which is known to reduce candida, fight bacteria and create a hostile environment for viruses.

Sugar feeds the growth of bad bacteria. When you are sick, you can replace grains and sugar in your diet with coconut oil as a natural fuel source. Instead of sugar, take one tablespoon of coconut oil three times daily and consume plenty of vegetables and bone broth.

7. Improves memory and brain function

In a study published in 2004 in the *Journal of Neurobiology of Aging*, researchers found that the MCFAs in coconut oil improved the memory loss in older subjects. There was a marked improvement across all the patients in recall ability after taking this fatty acid. As MCFAs are easily absorbed in the body and can be accessed in the brain without the use of insulin, they can fuel brain cells more efficiently.

8. Improves energy and endurance
Coconut oil is easy to digest, produces sustained energy and increases your metabolism. Quality unrefined coconut oil has the most benefits of coconut oil, and its MCFAs are sent directly to the liver to be converted into energy.

Today, many triathletes use coconut oil as their source of fuel during training and races and long-distance events. You can make an energy fuel at home by mixing coconut oil, raw honey and chia seeds. Simply put together one tablespoon of each and consume 30 minutes before exercising.

9. Improves digestion and reduces stomach ulcers and ulcerative colitis
Coconut also improves digestion as it helps the body absorb fat-soluble vitamins, calcium and magnesium. If coconut oil is taken at the same time as omega-3 fatty acids, it can make them twice as effective, as they are readily available to be digested and used by the body.

Coconut oil can help improve bacteria and gut health by destroying bad bacteria and candida. Candida imbalance can decrease stomach acid, which causes inflammation and poor digestion. All these benefits together mean coconut oil benefits digestive health and helps treat or prevent stomach ulcers and ulcerative colitis.

10. Improves skin issues such as burns, eczema, dandruff, dermatitis and psoriasis

Coconut oil is not only wonderful as a face cleanser, moisturiser and sunscreen but it can also treat many skin disorders. Fatty acids such as caprylic and lauric in coconut oil reduce inflammation internally and externally and moisturise the skin, which makes them a great solution for all types of skin conditions.

Coconut oil protects the skin and has many antioxidants that make it ideal for healing the skin. Also, the antimicrobial properties balance out the candida or fungal sources that can cause many skin conditions.

11. Prevents gum disease and tooth decay

Oil pulling with coconut oil has been used for centuries as a way to cleanse the mouth of bacteria and help cure periodontal disease. Coconut oil is one of the most effective oils for oil pulling thanks to its high concentration of antibacterial MCFAs.

Swishing the oil around in your mouth denatures the bacteria and sticks to them. Removing oral bacteria greatly reduces your risk of periodontal disease. If you want to heal your gums and repair your teeth, I recommend coconut oil pulling three times a week for 20 minutes a day.

12. Prevents osteoporosis

Oxidative stress and free radicals are the two biggest culprits of osteoporosis. Since coconut oil has such a high level of antioxidants that help fight free radicals, it is a leading natural treatment for osteoporosis.

Another amazing coconut oil benefit is that it increases calcium absorption in the gut. Research on osteoporosis has found that coconut oil not only increases bone volume and structure in subjects but also decreases bone loss due to osteoporosis.

13. Helps with type 2 diabetes

When cells refuse to respond to insulin and no longer take in glucose for energy, they're considered insulin resistant. The pancreas then pumps out more insulin to compensate for this lack and goes into an overproduction cycle. Insulin resistance is the precursor to type 2 diabetes.

The MCFAs in coconut oil help balance the insulin reactions in the cells and promote a healthy digestive process. They take off the strain on the pancreas and give the body a consistent energy source that is not dependent on glucose reactions, which can prevent insulin resistance and ultimately type 2 diabetes.

14. Coconut oil for weight loss

Because of the energy-creating abilities of coconut oil and the fact that it's a no-carb oil, it is no wonder that it is beneficial in losing weight. It helps burn fat and calories, decrease appetite and, in studies, was especially helpful in losing belly fat.

Coconut's ability to help shed fat has been well-established. It might seem counterintuitive to assume that eating coconut oil (a fat) will contribute to fat loss, but it is quite logical. The key to understanding this phenomenon lies in the multidimensional ability of the MCFAs to control a variety of physiological processes.

15. Coconut oil benefits for hair care
If you have dandruff or dry hair, coconut oil has the perfect fatty acids to help improve these conditions. There is so much coconut oil can do for hair. You can make homemade coconut lavender shampoo to improve your hair and use coconut oil directly as an all-natural hair conditioner.

To get rid of dandruff and thicken hair, massage one tablespoon of coconut oil mixed with ten drops of rosemary essential oil into your scalp for 3 minutes. Then shower 30 minutes later.

16. Candida and yeast infections
A study published in the journal *Antimicrobial Agents and Chemotherapy* found the capric acid and lauric acid in coconut oil made for an effective natural treatment for candida albicans and yeast infections.

To effectively kill candida and treat yeast infections, remove processed sugar and refined grains from your diet and consume plenty of healthy fats. Take one tablespoon of coconut oil three times daily as a supplement instead.

17. Coconut oil for anti-ageing
According to research published in the medical journal *Food and Function*, coconut oil improves antioxidant levels and can slow ageing. Coconut oil works by reducing stress on the liver and lowering oxidative stress.

Researchers have also found that coconut oil may support detoxification because of how it works with the liver. To naturally slow ageing, take one tablespoon of coconut oil with antioxidant-rich berries for breakfast. You can also apply it directly to the skin for additional benefits and to smoothen the skin.

18. Coconut oil for hormonal balance
Using coconut oil benefits your hormones as well! It may help naturally balance hormones because it's a great source of saturated fat, including lauric acid. Studies have found that coconut oil may be an excellent fat to consume during menopause and may also have positives effects on oestrogen levels.

It naturally balances hormones, reduces sugar and grain consumption and increases healthy fats from coconut, avocado, flax seeds and ghee. You can also consume other coconut forms, such as coconut butter or coconut water.

Ghee

Ghee has been traditionally used in abundance in India. We sometimes underestimate the power of our ancient superfoods and the wonders they can do to our body.

The best ghee you can use is Gir cow or A2 cow ghee. But if that's not accessible, you can use any cow ghee. Cow ghee has higher antioxidant content than buffalo ghee.

Some of the health benefits of ghee are described as follows.

1. Has a high burning point

This is the temperature at which an oil begins to burn and smoke. Not only does heating a cooking fat above its smoke point put it at a greater risk of hitting its flash point and causing a fire but it also breaks down important phytonutrients and causes the fat to oxidise and form harmful free radicals.

Unfortunately, most cooking oils with a high smoke point are less-than-stellar for your health. Canola oil, peanut oil, corn oil and soybean oil are usually genetically modified and also often partially hydrogenated to increase their stability.

Ghee, on the other hand, is an excellent choice for cooking because of its high smoke point and beneficial health effects. The smoke point of ghee is 485°F, which is much higher than the smoke point of butter at 350°F. This means that you can easily use ghee for baking, sautéing and roasting without the risk of destroying the important nutrients that it contains and that are behind all these wonderful ghee benefits.

2. Full of fat-soluble vitamins

Adding in a few portions of ghee into your day is the best way to consume some extra fat-soluble vitamins. This helps enhance your intake of vitamin A, vitamin E, vitamin K and all the imperative nutrients that play a role in everything from maintaining healthy eyesight to glowing skin.

This can be especially crucial if you suffer from any conditions such as leaky gut syndrome, IBS or Crohn's disease, as your body may have difficulty absorbing these fat-soluble vitamins. Ghee benefits your health by providing a boost of these nutrients to help you meet your daily needs.

3. No lactose and casein
One of the greatest benefits of ghee is that it's free of lactose and casein protein. Some individuals have a milk allergy, which may stem from a heightened sensitivity to casein, while others may be hypersensitive to lactose. For individuals with a casein allergy, the reaction to milk may include swelling of lips, mouth, tongue, face or throat, hives or congestion.

Those with lactose intolerance have a difficult time digesting milk sugar lactose, but symptoms are generally much less dangerous than in a casein allergy. Symptoms of lactose intolerance may include bloating, flatulence, nausea, vomiting, gurgling and cramps. Most people who are sensitive to either casein or lactose don't have an issue with ghee, as these elements have been removed through skimming and straining.

4. Contains conjugated linoleic acid
Ghee is jam-packed with conjugated linoleic acid (CLA), a fatty acid associated with a long list of health benefits. Some studies have found that CLA may be effective in reducing body fat, preventing cancer formation, alleviating inflammation and even lowering blood pressure.

5. Loaded with butyrate, or butyric acid
Ghee contains butyrate acid, which is a short-chain fatty acid that plays a central role in gut health. Some studies have suggested that it may help support healthy insulin levels, fight

off inflammation and provide relief for individuals suffering from conditions such as Crohn's disease and ulcerative colitis.

This important fatty acid is also made by the gut flora when you eat fibre. As the primary source of energy for the cells in your colon, butyrate is key to promoting a healthy gut microbiome, which plays an integral role in health and disease.

6. Contains vitamin K, vital for bone health

Regularly incorporating a few servings of ghee into your diet can help you meet your vitamin K needs. Vitamin K is essential to many aspects of health, such as blood clotting, heart health and brain function. It's also incredibly important when it comes to keeping your bones healthy and strong.

This is because vitamin K is directly involved in bone metabolism and increases the amount of a specific protein that is required to maintain the calcium in your bones.

Ghee supplies a small amount of vitamin K but can make a big difference when combined with an overall healthy diet and lifestyle, not to mention all the other ghee benefits you can get.

7. Medium-chain fatty acids promote healthy weight loss

The medium-chain fatty acids found in healthy fats such as ghee and coconut oil can boost fat burning and ramp up weight loss. A 2015 review comprising thirteen trials found that medium-chain triglycerides helped decrease body weight, waist and hip circumference, total fat and belly fat compared to long-chain triglycerides.

Not only that, but CLA, one of the primary fatty acids found in ghee, has been associated with reduced body fat mass as well.

Curious about how to use ghee for weight loss to achieve maximum results? Swap unhealthy fats such as vegetable oils with ghee, and try roasting, sautéing or baking your favourite healthy dishes to get the most of these ghee benefits.

8. Excellent source of butyrate which improves digestion

As mentioned above, ghee is an excellent source of butyrate, the short-chain fatty acid that is crucial to maintaining optimal digestive health. Butyrate provides energy for the cells in the colon, helps support gut barrier function and fights off inflammation.

Additionally, some studies have suggested that butyrate may provide relief from constipation. A review out of Poland, for example, noted that butyric acid reduces pain during defecation and improves peristalsis, or the contraction of muscles in the intestines, to help propel food through the digestive tract.

9. Butyrate also relieves inflammation

Although inflammation can be a normal immune response to defend the body against foreign invaders, long-term inflammation is believed to contribute to the development of the chronic disease.

As butyrate has been shown to inhibit inflammation in some test-tube studies, consuming ghee could help with this condition. This could have far-reaching benefits when it comes to preventing inflammatory conditions such as arthritis, inflammatory bowel disease, Alzheimer's, diabetes and even certain types of cancer.

Spirulina

This blue-green algae is a freshwater plant that is now one of the most researched and, alongside its cousin chlorella, most talked about superfoods today. Grown around the world from Mexico to Africa to Hawaii, spirulina is renowned for its intense flavour and even more powerful nutritional profile. There is too much scientific evidence of the nutritional value and health benefits of this superfood to give it a miss. To date, nearly 1,700 peer-reviewed scientific articles have evaluated its health benefits.

While you may have only seen it as an ingredient in your green superfood beverages, energy bars and natural supplements, spirulina benefits are so profound that they could help restore and revitalise your health when taken daily.

Spirulina is a biomass of cyanobacteria (blue-green algae) that can be consumed by humans and other animals. There are two species of spirulina: Arthrospira platensis and Arthrospira maxima. Both are cultivated worldwide and used as a dietary supplement (in tablet, flake and powder form) and as a whole food.

Health benefits of spirulina:

1. Detoxes heavy metals (especially arsenic)
Chronic arsenic toxicity is a profound challenge that is affecting people worldwide. According to the World Health Organization, the US is one of the countries affected by inorganic arsenic that is naturally present at high levels.

Spirulina is a great source of antioxidants and protects oxidative damage to the body. The main active component in spirulina, called phycocyanin, is an antioxidant that gives it its characteristic blue-green colour.

Phycocyanin fights free radicals and also restricts the production of inflammatory signalling molecules, thus having remarkable antioxidant and anti-inflammatory effects.

2. Eliminates candida
Spirulina against candida? Spirulina wins!

According to researchers, 'Candida species belong to the normal microbiota of an individual's mucosal oral cavity, gastrointestinal tract and vagina'. What does that mean? Well, without a healthy microflora balance in our body, we are simply much more susceptible to sickness and disease. In fact, leaky gut syndrome and improper digestion are directly connected to microflora imbalance. Both are caused by our shift towards a diet rich in sugar and unnatural ingredients, antimicrobial resistance and ineffective antifungal drugs. We have also seen a significant rise in yeast infections since the 1980s due to this.

Spirulina has shown good results in several studies on animals, where it has been an effective antimicrobial agent, particularly for candida. Specifically, spirulina benefits have been shown to promote the growth of healthy bacterial flora in the intestines, which in turn inhibits candida. Additionally, the immunity-strengthening properties of spirulina help the body eliminate candida cells.

3. Helps prevent cancer
According to the University of Maryland Medical Center, several animal and test-tube studies suggest that spirulina increases production of antibodies, infection-fighting proteins

and other cells that help ward off infection and chronic illnesses such as cancer.

Another article written in the Media graphics talks about the 'anti-cancer effects of blue-green alga Spirulina platensis, a natural source of bilirubin-like tetrapyrrolic compounds'. The study evaluated the possible anticancer effects of spirulina using an experimental model of pancreatic cancer. It showed that spirulina's potent antioxidant activity played the role of an inhibitor with potential for its broad use in the chemo adjuvant treatment of cancer diseases.

4. Lowers blood pressure

High blood pressure is the main reason behind a host of serious diseases such as strokes and chronic kidney ailments. Spirulina, also known as the 'most complete food in the world', does wonders to your heart by making it relax and thereby reducing the risk of strokes and heart diseases.

Phycocyanin is a pigment found in spirulina that scientists have found to possess antihypertensive effects (it lowers blood pressure). Japanese researchers claim that this is because consuming the algae reverses endothelial dysfunction in the metabolic syndrome.

Spirulina causes the artery to relax by a process that increases the blood pumped in one motion. This action is caused by nitric oxide, a chemical that helps keep healthy blood pressure.

5. Controls bad LDL and triglyceride levels

Various studies and research have been conducted all around the world to check the effects of spirulina in lowering bad LDL, triglycerides and BMI index. It was found that supplementing spirulina at 2–8 g/day could benefit lipid profiles, mainly by reducing TC, TG and LDL-c and improving HDL-c, aiding weight loss and reducing BMI.

This wonder food can also help keep your heart healthy as it contains niacin, a vitamin B3, and prevents dyslipidaemia, which is an abnormal accumulation of lipids in the body. So, having a dose of 1 gm daily has powerful effects on your lipid profiles.

6. Helps in liver detoxification

Spirulina is well-known as an alkaliser for the body and helps cleanse the liver. Many types of research have suggested spirulina as an alternative treatment for non-alcoholic fatty liver diseases and dyslipidaemic disorders.

It helps undo a lot of damage to the liver caused by medication. So, go ahead and mix it in your smoothies and juices generously and enjoy its powerful effects.

7. Increases energy levels

Low on energy? This superfood contains polysaccharides (rhamnose and glycogen) and essential fat (GLA) that helps boost energy levels. It postpones muscle fatigue, thereby reducing exhaustion, and helps stabilise energy levels.

It takes a while to get accustomed to the acquired taste, and if you think you can't slurp it down with your smoothies, then you can go for tablets. But believe me, it's worth the effort.

8. Helps improve memory
This product of aquaculture has been promoted worldwide as the food of the future. It is said to prevent oxidative damage to the brain by reducing the levels of a harmful protein that causes memory loss. Several studies found that spirulina reduced the inflammation to the brain that is the main cause of Parkinson's disease.

Turmeric (Haldi)

The turmeric root has been a staple of Ayurvedic medicine for more than 4,000 years, making it one of the oldest known medicines in human history. It has had both medicinal and religious significance and has been used in all Indian cuisine.

Turmeric contains more than 100 amazing chemical compounds. These can help treat conditions ranging from stomach aches to respiratory illnesses. These chemical compounds, along with curcumin, is what makes turmeric unique. Curcumin is what gives the turmeric root its beautiful yellow-orange colour. Curcuminoids, the group of chemical compounds responsible for the health benefits of turmeric, include curcumin, desmethoxycurcumin, and bisdemethoxycurcumin. Turmeric also contains volatile oils, including tumerone, artumerone and zingiberene.

Most importantly, turmeric also contains polyphenols, which are organic chemicals that have been shown to have anti-inflammatory properties. Polyphenols can be found in foods and beverages, such as epigallocatechin in green tea, capsaicin in chilli peppers and resveratrol in red wine and fresh peanuts.

Turmeric's unique chemical composition of vitamins, minerals, fibre and phytochemicals provide the following benefits:

- Building immunity
- Fortifying against illnesses
- Inhibiting the development of serious illnesses
- Obliterating cells that can cause serious illnesses within the body

1. Turmeric and overall health
The active compound in turmeric, curcumin, has many health benefits, from preventing cancer and Alzheimer's to heart diseases. It is full of antioxidants that are proven to improve symptoms of depression and arthritis.

2. Turmeric and skin
Turmeric is known to calm the skin, and its anti-inflammatory properties prevent and cure acne and related skin problems. Indian households have traditionally used turmeric as a paste for new-born babies, as soap can be too harsh for their delicate skin. Turmeric is very useful for adults too in bringing out natural skin glow and treat uneven skin tone.

3. Turmeric and hair
Compounds of turmeric can absorb vitamin D and encourage hair growth. Its anti-inflammatory properties help reduce dandruff and keep the scalp clean.

Turmeric also reinforces strength, conditioning and increased growth naturally and has been among the most sought-after DIY hair masks lately. Mix it with other natural ingredients to make your hair mask.

4. Turmeric and cold
Turmeric has been used by our forefathers generously in all food to improve immunity. It has been used in home remedies for the common cold as it helps break down mucus, thereby opening airways to your lungs. Recent studies have also found that curcumin inhibits COPD-like airway inflammation and also lung cancer. Turmeric can be used in fresh, dry and powdered form. So, include turmeric in all your preparations to enjoy its benefits.

5. Turmeric and menstruation
Considered to be among the top medicinal herbs in regulating menstruation and hormone problems in women, turmeric also has antispasmodic properties that help relieve menstrual pain. This natural pain reliever has been used very commonly during the menstrual cycle.

Collagen

You might recognise it as an ingredient in your favourite body lotion or perhaps notice supplements in the vitamin aisle that feature it. But what is collagen? What does collagen do, exactly? And how can you incorporate it into your life?

Collagen is found plentifully in our bodies as protein, particularly type 1 collagen. The word collagen is derived from a Greek word, where 'kola' means 'gum', and 'gen' means 'producing'. Collagen is a protein with a fibrous structure in the extracellular matrix and connective tissue of animals (Ramshaw et al., 2009). It is found in all parts of our body, such as muscle, bone, skin, blood vessels, the digestive system and tendons. Collagen is very beneficial, as it gives our skin strength and elasticity along with replacing dead skin cells. When it comes to our joints and tendons, in simplest terms, it's the 'glue' that holds the body together.

Our body naturally starts depleting its collagen reserves as we age. We can thank this degenerative process for signs of ageing, such as wrinkles, sagging skin and joint pains due to weaker or decreased cartilage (hello, skeleton legs). Other lifestyle factors such as eating a diet high in sugar, smoking and high amounts of sun exposure also contribute to lower collagen levels. It's been found that collagen-related diseases most commonly arise from a combination of either genetic defects, poor intake of collagen-rich foods, nutritional deficiencies or digestive problems affecting production (synthesis) of collagen.

Collagen is often called a 'complex protein', which is not surprising considering it contains a whopping total of nineteen different amino acids. These include a mix of both nonessential (also called conditional) and essential types. Collagen is a particularly great way to get more conditional amino acids, such as arginine, glutamine, glycine and proline.

The highest percentages of amino acids found within collagen, along with some of their key benefits, include the following:

1. Proline: Proline contributes to 15 per cent of collagen. Proline and glycine in particular play a major role in ensuring that your body runs smoothly. Proline helps protect the integrity of blood vessels, improve joint health and has various cardiovascular benefits.
2. Glycine: Glycine contributes to around one-third of the protein found in collagen. Though it's the smallest amino acid according to size, glycine has huge effects on the body. To ensure our cells function properly, glycine helps build healthy DNA strands. It's also one of three amino acids that form creatine, which promotes healthy muscle growth and boosts energy production during workouts.
3. Glutamine: One of the most important and abundant amino acids in the body, glutamine is both created within our muscles and also obtained from food sources. Research shows that glutamine helps prevent anxiety, tension, sleep disorders/insomnia, a lack of concentration, poor digestive health, a weakened immune system and low energy. According to a report printed the *American Journal of Clinical Nutrition*, it has been shown to have positive effects on the production of the growth hormone. This can improve aspects of mental health, such as helping with the release of GABA, which boosts feelings of 'inner calm and tranquillity'. Nitrogen, created by high amounts of glutamine, also helps with wound healing and prevents muscle wasting and joint pains.
4. Arginine: Arginine (also commonly called L-arginine) breaks down into nitric oxide within the body, which is an

important compound for arterial and heart health. Arginine has also been shown to improve circulation, help strengthen the immune system and have a positive influence on male libido.

Here are some of the health benefits of collagen:

1. Improves health of skin and hair
Collagen for skin? It's considered the No. 1 collagen benefit for a reason. As we age, collagen production declines. It's true and actually happening as you read this! You will notice it physically with more delicate and looser skin, more wrinkles and less elasticity. Higher collagen levels can help your skin look firmer, increase smoothness and help your skin cells keep renewing and repairing themselves normally.

Collagen benefits also include reducing cellulite and stretch marks. When skin loses its elasticity as a result of decreased collagen, there's another side effect: more visible cellulite. Because your skin is now thinner, cellulite becomes more evident—no more hiding what's happening below the surface. Collagen for skin helps its elasticity and helps reduce potential dimpling.

2. Reduces joint pains and degeneration
Have you ever felt like you've got 'skeleton legs', the kind that feel extra stiff and hurt when you move? Yup, that's likely collagen loss rearing its ugly head. That's because when we lose collagen, our tendons and ligaments start moving less easily, leading to stiffness, swollen joints and more problems.

With its gel-like smooth structure that covers and holds our bones together, collagen allows us to glide and move without pain. Think of ingesting more collagen like greasing a creaky door hinge: it helps your joints move more easily, reduces the pain often associated with ageing and even reduces the risk of joint deterioration. It's no surprise then that a recent study even found that collagen is an effective treatment for treating osteoarthritis and other joint pains and disorders.

Combined with calcium, collagen is necessary for those suffering from osteoarthritis and osteoporosis. It works to bind with calcium and control the weakening of bones. Calcium and collagen are generally used in combination to strengthen bones and improve flexibility.

3. Helps heal leaky gut

If you suffer from leaky gut syndrome, a condition where toxins that are bad for you can pass through your digestive tract, collagen can be super-helpful. It breaks down proteins and soothes your gut lining, healing damaged cell walls and infusing them with healing amino acids.

The biggest digestive benefit of consuming more collagen is that it helps form connective tissue and therefore 'seals and heals' the protective lining of the gastrointestinal tract. We know today that many illnesses can be traced back to inflammation or irritation stemming from an unhealthy gut. Poor gut health, including changes in the gut microbiome and permeability in the gut lining, allows particles to pass into the bloodstream where they can kick off an inflammatory cascade (hence the name leaky gut syndrome).

4. Strengthens nails, hair and teeth

Ever had peeling and splitting nails? Well, a lack of collagen could be to blame. The collagen protein is the building block of your fingernails, hair and teeth. Adding collagen to your diet regimen can help keep your nails strong and possibly reverse hair loss.

It is an excellent supplement for building natural proteins that not only strengthen weak and brittle nails but also play a major role in helping grow long and strong hair.

Collagen also helps bind our teeth together and keep our gums intact. Several studies have connected low collagen in our body to the loss of teeth as they are made up of collagen fibres that are in the connective tissues. So, to have a glowing smile, make sure that you are getting enough collagen.

5. Promotes healing of injuries

Collagen helps build connective tissues that promote strong muscles, skin and joints. It especially helps the regeneration of muscle mass lost in sports injuries. Keep your collagen levels high to help strengthen your bones, ligaments and cartilages.

6. Maintains cardiovascular health

Keep your heart naturally fit and healthy. Taking collagen can also help strengthen your blood vessels and improve circulation of blood. A strong heart and circulatory system keep all related diseases away and extend longevity.

Vegetarian and Non-vegetarian Bone Broth Recipes

Bone broth contains the collagen that is essential for rebuilding bone, connective tissue, and skin. Bone broth is especially beneficial in protecting our joints, aiding digestion and fighting inflammation.

Here are some easy recipes for bone broth to derive the benefits of collagen.

1. Vegetarians can boil bone broth collagen powder, ginger, cilantro, lime, cumin, black pepper and salt in water. Strain and drink.
2. You can also add wakame seaweed, shiitake mushrooms, coconut oil or olive oil, turmeric and spinach or kale to a large pot and boil for about an hour. Wakame seaweed is available in dried packages in health food stores and online. If you can't find it anywhere, you can use nori as a substitute.
3. The third veg recipe is a very easy-to-make broth with common household veggies. Boil the following vegetables in water: chopped fresh leafy greens, cabbage, kale, carrots, celery stalks, sweet potato, a fennel bulb halved, onions, leek roots, wakame (optional), fresh ginger, fresh turmeric, garlic cloves and bay leaves.
4. Non-vegetarian bone broth is made by simmering marrow-rich animal bones (beef, chicken, turkey, pork) for longer periods (often 12 hours on the stovetop) or pressure cooker for at least 3–4 hours. Once cooled, it looks like jelly because of its high gelatine content.

Ashwagandha

A lot is being spoken about ashwagandha, and people have now started realising how important this herb is. Ashwagandha is very important in Ayurveda and is mostly cultivated in Central India. In Sanskrit, 'ashwagandha' means 'the smell of a horse', which is because of its distinctive smell and its ability to build strength. It has now gained global recognition and multiple clinical studies have been undertaken to learn more about this wonder herb. Growing evidence is being collated around this powerful herb with a remarkable variety of health benefits.

Ashwagandha is also called the 'Indian winter cherry' or 'Indian ginseng' and has been part of a traditional system of medicine in India. It was a part of 'Rasayana', which is a herbal preparation to induce a youthful state of body and mind. Rasayana is an alternative medicine that works on the principles of natural healing and has been used for over 3,000 years to relieve stress and increase concentration.

Ashwagandha also contains alkaloids/withanolides that help build immunity and treat a host of mental illnesses. The roots and leaves of this herb are used widely in medicinal products.

Let us talk about some of the important benefits of ashwagandha.

1. Reduces blood sugar levels

Studies have revealed that this wonder herb helps reduce blood sugar levels of healthy individuals and diabetics alike. Insulin is a very important hormone that regulates glucose in our blood, and a lack of it over time causes a form of diabetes. Ashwagandha increases insulin secretion and thereby improves insulin sensitivity.

2. Helps reduce stress and anxiety

Stress and anxiety related to depression are on the rise, and people are dealing with it day in and day out. Here is a natural remedy that helps treat stress in a big way. A lot of research has been carried out on how ashwagandha helps block stress by controlling the signals in the nervous system. It has also reduced the symptoms of people dealing with stress.

Cortisol is a stress hormone that is released from our glands in response to a stressful situation. An overproduction of these hormones leads to high blood sugar levels and an increase in fat around the abdomen. Chronically stressed individuals have immensely benefitted from regularly taking ashwagandha supplements.

Take ashwagandha regularly as it helps bring out that rainbow in your life. It helps reduce the symptoms of depression and gives you a chance to feel happy.

3. Reduces inflammation in the body

Numerous studies have found that ashwagandha increases the activity of immune cells that act as natural painkillers and even fight infection. These immune cells also decrease inflammation such as C-reactive protein, which is linked to the risk of heart diseases.

Take this wonder herb called ashwagandha daily to pull your immune system up and fight infections naturally.

4. Fights neurodegenerative diseases

Withanamide, which is an active ingredient in ashwagandha, has shown to fight against B-amyloid-induced plaques in Alzheimer's disease. This natural oxidant scavenges free radicals in our brain to prevent cell damage and has also shown to protect against Parkinson's disease.

Our bodies are not meant to take continuous stress, which can be very detrimental to overall health. Taking supplements of ashwagandha has been found to support the adrenals that reduce the negative effects of high (or low levels) of this hormone.

Neem

The neem tree, Azadirachta indica, is probably India's best-kept secret! We all know about the powerful neem tree, and this legendary tree has been used since prehistoric times. India was envied for prized ingredients like saffron, turmeric, black pepper and silk. The British managed to take all these ingredients across the seas to Europe but failed to recognise the value of the neem tree. I am sure if they had known about this wonder herb, it would have been a worldwide phenomenon today.

Neem has powerful antibacterial and antifungal properties and is commonly used in skin, hair and a host of other treatments.

While some of us dread the thought of eating bitter neem leaves, this widely popular healing herb has uncountable benefits. Neem is known to have anti-bacterial, anti-fungal, anti-inflammatory and analgesic properties that not only benefit your health but also keep skin problems at bay. Every part of the neem tree has medicinal properties and has been used in therapeutic preparations.

There is also an indication that neem has been used as far as 4,500 years ago to support healing. Even today, the neem tree is valued as the 'dispensary', as every part of it possesses unique therapeutic properties.

Here are some of the benefits of neem:

1. Purifies blood
Neem is publicised as one of the best antiseptic, anti-viral and anti-bacterial agents. It helps purify the blood and thereby keeps your internal system clean. Its bitter taste has an incredible cooling property and helps reduce excess heat in the body. It removes the harmful toxins from the blood that disrupt the functioning of vital parts such as the liver and kidneys.

2. Heals skin
Your grandmother believed in the benefits of neem years ago. It has proven to be a miracle for people with skin problems. Neem is celebrated for promoting healthy and clear skin. Its skin benefits work both internally and externally. Neem oil promotes the healing of wounds and also keeps your skin healthy. Its anti-inflammatory properties help reduce acne and other skin-related issues. It contains vitamin C, which helps reduce dullness and ageing of the skin. Neem is also known to reduce skin itchiness and redness.

3. Builds immunity
Research suggests that neem boosts both the lymphocytic and cell-mediated immune systems to help build immunity in the

body. The detoxifying effects of neem make it a great immune booster. So, build your immunity by including neem in your daily supplements.

4. Stabilises glucose
The WHO has claimed that by the year 2030, diabetes will be the seventh-largest killer globally. Diabetes is a protracted metabolic disease categorised by elevated levels of blood glucose (or blood sugar) that can seriously damage the heart, blood vessels, eyes, kidneys and nerves.

Studies have found that certain compounds of neem benefit diabetes mellitus. According to a study published in the *Indian Journal of Physiology and Pharmacology*, neem may also prove helpful in preventing or delaying the onset of the disease. In the journal *Studies on Ethno-Medicine*, neem leaf powder was found to control diabetic symptoms on non-insulin-dependent male diabetics. Neem has also helped support healthy blood sugar levels already in the normal range.

5. Improves digestive health
A healthy digestive system is very important for overall health. Neem promotes a healthy digestive system by protecting the stomach against indigestion and heartburns. It also helps eliminate toxins from the body and reduces the concentration of excess acids in the body.

6. Helps with weight management
Neem assists in the breakdown of body fat by improving your body's metabolism and keeping your weight in check. Try

mixing neem with lemon and honey to boost your metabolism and see the effects.

Neem also has kapha-reducing properties that encourage your body to properly digest and eliminate fat and water. This prevents water retention in the body.

Berries

Berries are among some of the healthiest foods to eat. Not only are they delicious but also provide a host of very impressive health benefits. Loads of different types of berries are available, but some of the most known berries are blueberries, raspberries, goji berries, strawberries, bilberries, acai berries, cranberries and grapes.

The word 'berry' is derived from the old English word 'berie', which meant 'grape'. As the English language spread across the world, many native grape-like fruits took on the '-berry' suffix. So, we now have blueberry, elderberry and so on.

Today berries are widely marketed as the new superfood that instantly brings up energy levels and puts a glow on your face. Using berries in combination with other foods also helps derive the benefits of this super fruit! Besides eating them plain, you can also add them fresh or frozen or other high-nutrition foods such as yoghurt, oatmeal and salads.

Here are some of the health benefits of berries:

1. Loaded with antioxidants
When free radicals multiply very fast in the body and go beyond the health requirement, they form oxidative stress. Berries are

loaded with antioxidants such as anthocyanins, ellagic acid and resveratrol, which play an important role in keeping oxidative stress under control.

2. Rich in fibre
Berries are a good source of high fibre, which also includes soluble fibre. This helps reduce hunger by making you feel full faster. The benefits of this are that it helps lower your calorie intake and keep your weight in check. High fibre also means that they are lower in net carbohydrates, which also helps control your weight. So, go ahead and have these wonder fruits in plenty.

3. High nutritional value
Berries contain several vitamins and minerals such as vitamin C, manganese, vitamin K1, copper and folate. This provides your body with holistic nutritional value. These fruits are known to provide you with a host of benefits from cell protection to iron absorption and also help the transmission of nerve and muscle signals.

4. Keeps your heart healthy
Endothelial cells are found in the lining of your blood vessels and help control blood pressure. Excessive inflammation can inhibit proper functioning of these cells, which is also a major reason for heart diseases. Studies have revealed that berries improve the functioning of endothelial cells and have also cured inflammation.

5. Boosts mental health

Berries contain antioxidants that help fight the effects of age on the brain. Data reported from the American Chemical Society suggests that berries contain chemical compounds called polyphenolics, which could help prevent Alzheimer's disease by cleaning up the damaging build-up of toxins over time.

People who eat at least two servings of berries a week have a 25 per cent less chance of developing Parkinson's disease than their peers, according to research published in the journal *Neurology*. The same research showed that men with the highest intake of flavonoids, which are abundant in berries, reduced their risk by 40 per cent.

6. Fights urinary tract infection

Berries encourage urinary tract health and protect against infection with an important compound that helps fight bacteria and keeps it from sticking to the lining of the urinary tract. So eat a lot of berries and keep UTI at bay!

Nuts and Seeds

Evidence shows that nuts have been a part of the main diet of humans since the beginnings of history. Researchers recently found an assortment of nuts with stone tools hidden deep in a bog in Israel. Back then, nuts were eaten as a source of energy, but now we know that they are also a good source of proteins, healthy fats, vitamins and minerals. A lot of research has been conducted on the effect of nuts and seeds on the heart, and it was found that it lowers the risk of diabetes and heart-related diseases. Some of the different nuts available are pistachios, hazelnuts, cashew nuts, walnuts, almonds, peanuts, pine nuts and pecans. Sunflower seeds, pumpkin seeds, hemp seeds, chia seeds, flax seeds and sesame seeds are some of the well-known seeds with loads of nutritional value. The FDA now allows nut producers to claim that a diet that includes one ounce of nuts daily can reduce your risk of heart disease.

How do you ensure a daily intake of nuts and seeds?

Nuts eaten raw or roasted are the best way to retain nutrition in them, as processing could strip them of their nutritional value. Ensure that you get at least 1.5 oz of nuts or seeds per day. The best way to ensure that you have a regular intake of nuts is by keeping them handy as a snack. You can also have them as spreads, which are available in supermarkets, sprinkle them in your cereals, sandwiches and salads or use them in place of processed meats. Always remember to read the label to check for added salt and sugar, which are not recommended.

Here are some of the benefits of eating nuts:

1. Balance lipid profiles
Nuts are full of unsaturated fats that help lower bad cholesterol (LDL) and increase good cholesterol. Nuts contain omega-3 fatty acids that lower the level of triglycerides in the blood and slow down the growth of plaque in the arteries. It also prevents erratic heart rhythms and blood clots, which are the primary reason for strokes.

2. Reduce inflammation

Nuts have known to have robust anti-inflammatory properties. Chronic long-term inflammation can increase damage to the organs and expose us to diseases.

In a study on the Mediterranean diet, people whose diets were supplemented with nuts experienced a 35 per cent and 90 per cent decrease in the inflammatory markers C-reactive protein (CRP) and interleukin 6 (IL-6), respectively. Similarly, some nuts, including pistachios, Brazil nuts, walnuts and almonds, have been found to fight inflammation in healthy people and those with serious conditions such as diabetes and kidney disease.

3. Keep you feeling full

Nuts are very rich in good fat, protein and fibre. This helps you feel full for a longer time and also maintain your weight. The unique nutrient profiles of nuts and seeds help in weight regulation, controlling obesity and related conditions. Most nut types are high in monounsaturated fats and polyunsaturated fats (mainly walnuts), which are good for the heart. Some nuts are also a good source of an amino acid called L-arginine that helps you burn fat. Eating a handful of nuts or seeds will keep the bad fat at bay and also boost your immunity.

4. Control sugar levels

Nuts are one of several foods that the American Diabetes Association lists as beneficial for people with the condition. Recent studies have revealed that people who consumed nuts daily had their blood sugar level under control, which decreased their risk of resultant heart disease. Eating nuts helps raise the level of glucagon-like peptide 1, which is a hormone that lowers insulin levels and controls blood sugar.

Seeds

People have now started realising the importance of seeds in their diet. Seeds are a great source of fibre and are packed with healthy monounsaturated fats, polyunsaturated fats and many important vitamins, minerals and antioxidants. They are also rich in trace minerals such as selenium, magnesium, copper and zinc, which are very crucial for our bodies.

Seeds are as beneficial as their glamorous cousins, the nuts, but have come into the limelight only lately.

1. Dense in nutrients
Seeds are full of good fats, complex carbohydrates, proteins, vitamins and fibre. They can give you a really big boost in energy and also are nourishing in the long run.

2. Help keep the digestive system on track
The high fibre content in seeds helps slow down digestion and keeps digestion woes at bay.

3. Keep you physically and mentally fit
The good fats in seeds help nourish blood cells and maintain brain function. If consumed regularly over time, seeds can help prevent weight gain.

4. Reduce risk of heart disease

Seeds are also very beneficial in reducing inflammation. They contain plant sterols, which help keep cholesterol levels in check and heart diseases away.

Here are some easy ways to include nuts and seeds in your diet:

1. The Indian chikki or brittle is a traditional recipe commonly found in every household. Seeds and nuts chikki can be made with healthy sunflower and pumpkin seeds, nuts and palm sugar (jaggery). It is a power-packed and healthy substitute to the traditional peanut gajjak or chikki.
2. An easier way to ensure that you include nuts and seeds in your diet is to sprinkle a handful on toast, salads, scrambled eggs, tofu or tempeh.
3. Smoothies are an excellent source of energy and can also be carried on the go. They serve as a cool and delicious meal-in-a-glass. Nuts provide the necessary protein and good fat and also boost your omega-3 intake. Adding walnuts, almonds and peanuts with ground flax seeds to your smoothie is a sure way to keep your heart healthy.
4. The traditional Indian ladoo has always been a favourite during festivals. Here is a sure way to make it a tasty option in festivities. Oats and dry fruit ladoos with jaggery are a very good nutritious option for kids and adults alike. You could also try different healthy flours such as nachni as a substitute.

10

Reclaiming Our Roots: The Natural Approach to Good Health

---•---

Herbal teas have been around from time immemorial. There is evidence that our ancestors made infusions with all kinds of roots, herbs and parts of plants found in their immediate environment. Ancient Egypt and China have also recognised herbal teas as having medical benefits.

As long back as in the first century AD, the renowned Greek physician Pedanius Dioscorides introduced over 600 medicinal plants that could be soaked in water to make infusions with healing properties. Modern researchers have dug out dried peppermint leaves from the pyramids in Egypt that date back to 1000 BC.

Prehistoric records also show that herbal infusions were also used to induce a sense of calm and spiritual mindfulness. These days, people have started taking to herbal teas for their delightful taste and fragrance.

SO WHAT ARE HERBAL TEAS?

As the name suggests, these are not technically teas. Tea is made from Camellia sinensis, a plant used to produce black, oolong, green, and white teas. Herbal teas can be made from dried fruits, flowers, spices or herbs of non-tea plants. In India, this concoction is called 'kadha', while in Europe and other parts of the world, they are generally known as 'tisanes'.

Herbal teas have recently gained popularity due to their vibrant flavours as well as their countless mental, emotional and physical health benefits. With the increase in global stress levels, herbal teas take us back to our roots and shift the focus to wellness through a complete approach. The practice of using dried herbs, flowers, fruits, barks and other ingredients for achieving wellness continues today and supports a healthy mind and body.

Herbal teas such as chamomile, peppermint, rooibos and hibiscus are caffeine-free. These are good options for people who are hypersensitive to caffeine. But that does not stop coffee lovers from having a herbal tea concoction at any time of the day.

How do you make herbal tea?

To make herbal tea, a teaspoon of herbal tea leaves needs to be steeped for 5–7 minutes in boiling water. You can experiment with steeping times and tea concentrations to arrive at your preferred taste.

What are some of the common herbal tea varieties?

1. Peppermint tea
Peppermint tea is a very commonly made preparation that has myriad benefits from resolving digestive issues to providing antioxidant, antibacterial and antiviral properties to the body. Studies have reported that peppermint tea helps relieve IBS and relax intestinal spasms.

2. Chamomile tea
Chamomile tea is sourced from the chamomile flower that is known for its calming benefits and sleep-inducing properties. Several studies have found that it has a relaxing effect on the mind. The antioxidants found in chamomile play a major role in reducing your risk of several diseases, including heart disease and cancer.

3. Turmeric tea
Turmeric tea helps in easing arthritis symptoms, preventing Alzheimer's disease and cancer, maintaining ulcerative colitis remission, lowering bad cholesterol levels and boosting the immune system. You can mix turmeric and honey and preserve this paste. Mix one teaspoon of this paste for one cup of water, and add to it some black pepper. Give a final squeeze of lime, and your tea is ready!

4. Hibiscus tea
Hibiscus tea is packed with antioxidants that help lower blood pressure, reduce blood fat and help lose excess weight. Hibiscus is known to boost liver health and also fight bacteria. Hibiscus tea has a sweet and tart taste that is unique and refreshing.

5. Ginger tea
Ginger tea is a good source of antioxidants and helps to build immunity. A cup of herbal ginger tea relieves pain and aids in relaxing the muscles. It also helps lower stress and tension and plays an important role in calming your nerves. Have a concoction of ginger tea and honey to get rid of cold, cough and nasal congestion.

6. Red rooibos tea
People who would like to avoid the caffeine content present in regular tea and coffee can opt for rooibos tea. This tea is had as a substitute for black or green tea and is very rich in antioxidants, providing many benefits for the heart and liver.

Closer to home

Herbal teas, also known as 'kadhas' in India, have been extremely popular in our country for many generations. So let's use our age-old knowledge to boost our immunity and also achieve great health. You can drink kadha on an empty stomach in the morning or at any time of the day. You can have it 1–3 times a day.

Here's a recipe of my favourite immunity-boosting kadha or herbal tea:

Herbal tea recipe 1

Ingredients:

5–6 fresh tulsi leaves/2 tsp tulsi powder
½ inch grated ginger/ginger powder/sunth
1 tsp ajwain
1 tsp cardamom powder
½ tsp black pepper
1 tsp cinnamon powder
½ tsp turmeric
2 tsp green tea leaves
1 tsp organic jaggery/liquid jaggery/date jaggery

Process:

Add all the ingredients to 500 ml water and boil together for 10–15 minutes.

Strain the tea in a cup and squeeze a fresh lemon into the cup.

Sip on this super delicious and super powerful immunity herbal tea/kadha.

Herbal tea recipe 2

Ingredients:

1 tsp black tea
1 tsp green tea
1 stick cinnamon

1 cardamom
1 tsp ajwain
1 tsp sauf
½ tsp haldi
1 inch ginger
1 garlic clove
Lemongrass
Tulsi leaves
Pudina leaves

Process:

Boil all the ingredients together for 30 minutes or more.
Then add organic jaggery to the pot.
When the mixture cools down, squeeze one lemon into your cup.

Health benefits of Dr Rohini's immunity herbal tea/kadha:

- Kadha/herbal tea is a blended decoction useful against flu and infections.
- It is a decoction made from edible herbs and spices.
- Kadha can work wonders for your immunity.
- It regulates blood sugar levels.
- It helps combat respiratory ailments symptoms such as asthma, bronchitis, flu, cold, sore throat and sinusitis.
- It helps in gut healing and improving overall gut health.

What are the benefits of the spices used in herbal teas?

Cinnamon (Dalchini)
Cinnamon is derived from the inner bark of the cinnamon tree. It is full of antioxidants and has high anti-inflammatory properties. It controls metabolism and is critical for transporting blood sugar from your bloodstream to your cells.

Cardamom (Elaichi)
Cardamom is helpful for people with high blood pressure. It has a high level of antioxidants. Moreover, it also has a diuretic effect that removes excessive water retention in the body.

Carom seeds (Ajwain)
Carom seeds are very common in all Indian households. The spice is derived from a herb plant that belongs to our own country. Carom seeds serve two purposes: (i) bringing flavour to food; and (ii) having positive health effects. Carom seeds are good for digestive health and treat any abdominal uneasiness due to indigestion like stomach pain or a burning sensation in the stomach. It also helps increase the appetite for those suffering from a loss of appetite.

Fennel seeds (Saunf)
Fennel seeds are also called saunf in Hindi, and it is a fragrant herb derived from the parsley family. It is used as a spice and also possesses a sweet taste. Fennel seeds are high in fibre, which decreases the re-absorption of cholesterol and helps prevent

heart-related diseases. It is also a good source of potassium, vitamin C, iron and folic acid, thereby lowering the risk of anaemia and other immunity concerns. Having fennel tea twice a day regularly can improve breast milk production in nursing mothers apart from cleansing out accumulated toxins from the body.

Turmeric (Haldi)
Turmeric has been used for thousands of years as a medicinal herb. It has also been a common spice in Indian households. Turmeric contains curcumin, which has powerful anti-inflammatory and antioxidant effects. It helps our body fight infections. Curcumin also reduces the risk of brain diseases such as Alzheimer's disease, depression and even improves memory.

Ginger (Adrak)
Ginger is full of nutrients and bioactive compounds that have potent benefits for your body and brain. Ginger contains gingerol, which is a bioactive compound with powerful anti-inflammatory and antioxidant effects. Ginger is very effective in treating nausea due to seasickness, chemotherapy, after surgery and even morning sickness. Ginger also help treat stomach ailments and is soothing for the stomach. It also reduces muscle pain and may reduce exercise-induced muscle soreness.

Garlic (Lasun)
Garlic is low in calories while being high in its nutritional value. It is rich in vitamin C, vitamin B6 and manganese and also some amounts of other nutrients. Garlic helps prevent and also

reduce the severity of the common cold. It not only improves cases of high blood pressure but also helps maintain an optimum level of the blood pressure. Garlic has a lot of benefits for the heart as well and helps control cholesterol levels.

One of the main reasons for which herbal tea has been so readily accepted is that it gives you the benefits of herbs while also allowing the flexibility to try various combinations of herbs, spices and plants. These teas are also easy to make and consume. Eating the same herbs and spices in their raw form can be very gross for people. Drinking the same while mixing them with your favourite spice is much more acceptable and enjoyable. Other than being delicious, herbal teas also have healing properties that push people to try them.

Health benefits of herbal teas:

1. Fight common cold and flu
Herbal teas help in treating the common cold and soothing the throat. They help clear the nasal passage and also reduce coughing. Studies have also found that they help in managing the symptoms of asthma.

2. Improve digestive issues
Herbal teas help clear out the fat in the stomach, thereby reducing symptoms of indigestion. This further reduces the feeling of bloating and nausea. Some teas that treat these symptoms are chamomile, cinnamon, peppermint and ginger tea.

3. Boost immunity
Herbal teas are very rich in antioxidants that help fight diseases and infections. These also protect against oxidative stress, thereby lowering your risk of developing chronic diseases. Some of the best herbal teas for boosting your immune system include ginger and liquorice root tea.

4. Reduce inflammation
Herbal teas help people with inflammatory illnesses. It is known to reduce pain, tiredness and swelling in joints. Ginger is consumed to relieve inflammation, and when consumed in teas, it is the perfect treatment for joint and muscle pain.

5. Relieve stress and anxiety
Herbal teas calm and relax the mind and are the ideal drink before one goes to sleep. They helps cure insomnia and are great for relieving stress and anxiety. Chamomile tea is one of the best teas for stress relief and inducing sleep. The calming effect also acts as a mild anti-depressant as it curbs negative feelings.

6. Slow down ageing
Herbal teas are loaded with antioxidants that prevent free radical damage, thereby reduce the ageing of cells. This makes your skin and hair look and feel younger.

7. Lower blood pressure
Studies have revealed that herbal teas help lower one's blood pressure. Herbal teas such as hibiscus can decrease blood pressure without causing any negative side effects. High blood pressure

is known to heavily affect the heart and kidney. Hibiscus tea is a natural way to protect these from harm.

8. Detox the liver
Herbal teas are also called detox teas that help flush the body system and expel toxins from your internal organs. Calendula, also called 'sunshine in a cup', helps detoxify the digestive system while also giving you a nice dose of vitamin C.

9. Calm your intestines
Herbal teas help cure intestinal issues, especially those with digestion, nausea and acid reflux and they soothe the stomach. Ginger root helps in digestion (that's why we find it in our after-dinner mint tea). Lemon tea is known to relieve gas and bloating and to stimulate the digestive tract.

10. Great for healthy skin
Herbal tea is a natural treatment for acne. The tea can either be ingested normally or can be directly applied onto the skin. Rooibos and chamomile tea are the finest teas for healing and treating the skin due to their antioxidant and antibacterial properties. Spearmint tea also reduces acne breakouts.

SECTION TWO: TIPS

11

The Lifestyle Diet

Our fitness and wellbeing are directly linked to our lifestyle, and people have started realising that it works the inside-out way. A healthy lifestyle is the key to unlocking a healthier and fitter you. They say that you are what you eat. Better still, you are what you don't eat.

Here are some do's and don'ts to help you sail through a holistically healthy life.

1. Have these morning and night concoctions.
Organic, raw and unfiltered ACV/half a lemon in plain water (wheatgrass powder optional), digestive tea, chamomile tea.

2. Follow the suggested intermittent fasting plans.
The research on intermittent fasting is overwhelmingly positive, and not just from a fat-loss perspective. A few recent studies

have found that intermittent fasting also helps bring down the risk of coronary heart disease and diabetes as well as helps maintain blood cholesterol levels in healthy and pre-diabetic populations. It also contributes to longevity.

3. Never skip breakfast.
Have my favourite butter coffee for breakfast and feel energised. Butter coffee can be made with coffee, ghee, coconut oil, collagen powder (optional) and turmeric. Enjoy the many benefits of these ingredients.

4. Keep your dinners light.
You should have your dinners before 7:30 p.m. (4–5 hours before sleeping). Have a protein-rich diet along with veggies.

5. Meditate for at least 20 minutes every day.
Pick a quiet corner, sit and focus on your breathing. It is as simple as that. It has a very calming and relaxing effect and also aids overall well-being.

6. Do some form of exercise.
Do any form of exercise that suits your body and that you are comfortable. It could include walking, high-intensity interval training (HIIT), pilates, yoga, swimming or playing a sport. Try introducing a new workout form every six months.

7. Keep yourself hydrated.
Try to drink at least 3–4 litres of water every day. Tea and coffee are not included in this. In it you could squeeze a lemon,

soak fenugreek seeds or even try something exotic to make the experience more enjoyable.

Eating the right food at the right time goes a long way in maintaining a healthy lifestyle. Here are some healthy food options with the best time at which to consume them.

Food item	Breakfast	Lunch	Dinner
Eggs	Yes	Yes	Yes
Oats upma	Yes	No	No
Daliya	Yes	Yes	No
Dry fruits	Yes	Yes	Yes
Idli/dosa	Yes	Yes	No
Dal	No	Yes	Yes
Bhakari/chapati	Yes	Yes	No
Stuffed paratha	Yes	Yes	No
Salad or veggies	No	Sometimes	Yes
Stir-fry veggies	Yes	Yes	Yes
Buckwheat or whole-grain pasta	No	Yes	Yes
Green leafy vegetables, broccoli, tofu, mushrooms, paneer, dals, sprouts	Yes	Yes	Yes
Fruits	Yes	Yes	No
Quinoa or millets	Yes	Yes	Yes
Sprouts of different grains	Yes	Yes	Yes

Here are some additional notes:

1. Two whole eggs with yolk are compulsory for breakfast.
2. You can stuff your parathas with mushroom, sweet potatoes, palak, paneer, peas and so on.
3. Buckwheat or whole-grain pasta is always preferable in tomato sauce.
4. Strictly avoid fruits after 5 p.m.
5. Preferred oils for cooking include cold-pressed coconut oil, cold-pressed groundnut oil and organic cow ghee.

SNACKING

Snacking has acquired a bad image because of some people who consider it an unnecessary exercise of increasing our calorie intake. However, snacking in the right way can decrease hunger pangs and can also avoid poor food choices and excess intake of empty calories.

It is also useful in energising you before a workout and can also supplement your nutrition. Here are some nutritional options to keep stacked at home:

1. Bhel (homemade)
Make your bhel with baked varieties of the ingredients and also add fruits such as pomegranate for the extra zing. Squeeze in a lime and you are ready to soak in your dose of vitamin C for the day.

2. Roasted mixed seeds
This is a very healthy snack that gives you all the vitamins and minerals and can easily be carried in a small pouch/jar when you travel.

3. Makhanas
In the crazy rush to follow unhealthy eating habits such as junk food binging, we have forgotten makhanas, which take us back to our roots. This snack is economical, easy to make and very nutritious.

4. Nuts
Nuts are a good source of healthy fats, fibre and have loads of nutritional value. They also provide us with rich plant-based proteins which are especially beneficial for vegans.

5. Flavoured or regular hot coffee (no sugar; add stevia instead)
Coffee has the highest quantity of antioxidants that are very beneficial for the body. It helps you stay focussed and alert. Coffee also helps to burn bad fat and aids weight loss. This thereby lowers the risk of other mental and physical illnesses. Avoid sugar in your coffee though, as it nullifies its benefits. If you must have your coffee sweet, try stevia. This is easily available in all supermarkets.

6. Dark chocolate
Dark chocolate is very nutritious with high doses of fibre, iron, magnesium, copper, zinc, potassium and selenium. Studies also

show that the flavanols from dark chocolate improve blood flow to the skin.

7. Home-made ladoos

Our grandmothers' recipes of healthy ladoos are here to stay. Mix all the healthy flours (avoid refined flours) with ghee and jaggery and voilà! Ladoos made out of this can also be stored for longer durations. Being rich in calcium and magnesium, they help fortify and support the bone tissues.

8. Buttermilk (homemade)

Buttermilk, also called 'chaas' in India, makes for the most delightful drink in summer. It aids digestion and prevents acidity and heartburns. It is easily digestible and has a host of nutritional benefits.

9. Mixed dry fruits

Dry fruits are the easiest to consume with little or no preparation time. Add them as toppings on your food, grind to a paste to add to your food or simply eat them as they are. They are instant energy and mood boosters. Always carry them with you to satisfy your hunger pangs.

10. All types of herbal teas

I have spoken at length in my chapter on herbal teas, but I can't speak enough to fully cover all the benefits. These teas have wide-ranging benefits and can cure and even prevent just about any issue.

11. Ghee coffee

Ghee coffee is among my top favourite beverages. It has all the benefits of coffee, ghee, coconut oil and turmeric mixed in one drink. Have it first thing in the morning to feel energized and full instantly.

Trust me, staying away from certain foods can be testing, especially if they are designed to taste good. But they offer little to no nutritional value and can give rise to lifestyle-related diseases in the long run.

Here is a list of foods that you should avoid:

1. Maida

Maida is refined flour that has no nutritional value. It is derived from wheat but loses all its important fibre in the making process. Maida is known to increase the bad cholesterol in the body and also disrupt blood sugar levels. It doesn't satisfy your hunger and invariably causes mood swings. Substitute maida with other whole-grain flours such as jowar, bajra and nachni.

2. All processed and packaged foods

Processed and packaged foods are made with cheap ingredients to reduce the cost of production. They contain oils that are high in trans fats and promote the formation of free radicals in our body leading to excess oxidation and inflammation. These products also contain an excess of salt and sugar, which can worsen heart problems. The products are also contain a lot of preservatives to keep them fresh, which can have harmful side effects.

3. Dairy and dairy products except for curd and buttermilk (temporarily for four months)

Several studies have proved that dairy products are very high in saturated fat, which is a big contributor to heart disease, type 2 diabetes and Alzheimer's disease. Saturated fat has also been linked to breast, ovarian and prostate cancers. Substitute dairy products with almond milk or any other form of nut milk to get better benefits.

4. Refined sugar

Our body breaks down refined sugar faster, thereby pushing up the insulin and blood sugar to abnormal levels. Refined sugar is also digested faster and does not give satiety. This results in overconsumption and increases your calorie intake. Refined sugar also gives rise to a host of health issues such as obesity and belly fat and high-risk diseases such as diabetes and heart problems. Switch to natural sugars like jaggery or artificial sweeteners like stevia.

5. Gluten (temporarily)

Gluten is a protein found in the grain family, especially wheat, that forms a sticky, glue-like consistency and gives the dough its elasticity and chewy texture. It gives rise to a lot of issues of the digestive tract such as stomach pain, IBS, diarrhoea, bloating and also tiredness. Substitute gluten foods with non-gluten foods such as amaranth, buckwheat, rice, millet and quinoa among many other available options.

6. Deep-fried foods

Deep-fried foods are high in calories, and studies have found that eating fat-laden food can raise bad cholesterol levels and cause heart diseases. These foods are also usually full of excess salt, which can result in high blood pressure problems. Grilling, toasting or air frying are some healthier options.

HOW DO YOU MAINTAIN A HEALTHY LIFESTYLE?

Having a healthy lifestyle entails being mentally and physically fit. It prevents the onset of chronic illnesses and keeps you fighting fit. Feeling good is very important for your confidence and also acts as a big morale booster. Always remember to follow a healthy lifestyle by doing what is right for your body.

Here are a few things that you can do for yourself to retain that spring in your step:

1. Exercising

Exercising is known to release happy hormones in the body. These improve your overall emotional well-being and keep you balanced. Exercise also helps in weight loss while increasing your energy levels and reducing the risk of chronic diseases.

Try walking, jogging, weight training or body weight exercises (Three days a week! Must do!), yoga, tai chi or any favourite workout.

2. Meditation

Meditation is very well known the world over. It helps naturally treat depression and anxiety-related issues. It also helps strengthen your immunity and control chronic problems such as blood pressure and heart diseases. Meditating for 15–20 minutes daily induces a sense of calm and relaxation. Practice any form of meditation or practice gratitude for 10 minutes daily to see the difference. Maintaining a gratitude journal helps you reaffirm the things you need to be grateful for while also setting goals to make your life better.

3. Maintain a healthy lifestyle

You are responsible for yourself and your health. Always remember to keep it simple. Focus on the holistic approach to good health and never take your body for granted. Keep your diet as simple as you can while ensuring that you include all the healthy foods we read about earlier. Avoid eating food that can harm your body in the long run. I have given an exhaustive list of that too. Most importantly, ensure that you balance your food habits with a comfortable exercise regime. Exercising will keep your engine (your body) well-oiled and running. Keep your soul happy by meditating daily and avoiding unnecessary stress.

4. The most important one … Always stay happy, grateful and blessed!

Practising gratitude brings in a sense of satisfaction. 'What I have is enough for me' is the new mantra. Life has been kind and given us enough. It's even more important to be grateful for the health and fitness you've achieved so far and continue on the same path of gratitude.

CASE STUDY 2	
Client profile	• Age: 47 years • Weight: 96.3 kg • Height: 5 ft. 3 in.
Medical complications	• Diabetes, hypertension, obesity
Other complaints/ requirements	• The client suffered bouts of exhaustion and had trouble sleeping at night. She had sweet cravings. • She wished to lose weight.
Existing diet and exercise routine	• Largely home-cooked food • Eating out once a week • No exercise routine
Diet changes recommended	• Reduced intake of processed and fatty foods • Refined sugar and salt substituted with jaggery and rock/sea salt • Inclusions in diet: complex carbohydrates through millets, chillas and dosas; wholesome soups, salads and different types of khichdi, fish and chicken • Dinner time fixed at 7 pm • Refer to diet plan no. 46

CASE STUDY 2	
Exercise routine recommended	• Light walking and exercises (after considerable weight loss)
Other recommendations	• Reading affirmations • Meditation • Gratitude journaling
Improvement in condition	• Weight loss in the first four months: 96.3 kg to 87.2 kg • HbA1c reduced from 6.6 (diabetic) to 6.1 (pre-diabetic)

12

The Lifestyle Anti-ageing Diet

You are never too old to set another goal or dream a new dream. – *C.S. Lewis*

HEALTH AND BEAUTY should both come from the inside. I am sure that you want to look young and have soft, smooth and glowing skin. While the markets are full of expensive creams and lotions claiming to be the elixirs for good skin, you must also focus on food that provides the right combination of vitamins and minerals.

Vitamin and mineral deficiencies can make your skin look tired, wrinkled and blemished, discoloured or hyper-pigmented in areas. Vitamins and minerals are also crucial for proper physical and mental functioning.

Anti-ageing has been in focus for some time now, and people in their early thirties have also begun to take anti-ageing seriously. People have become conscious about living healthy to improve longevity. Anti-ageing is an important component of a healthy living.

BUT WHAT IS ANTI-AGEING?

Anti-ageing is the slowing down, preventing and, to some extent, reversing of the ageing process. The rise in life expectancy witnessed in the twentieth century has made ageing and longevity important topics.

You would be happy to know that you can reverse some of the damage caused to your body by increasing the intake of vibrant foods loaded with antioxidants and healthy fats and reducing toxic foods such as sugar and processed foods, among many more that promote ageing.

Here are some things that you need to include in your diet and some practices you need to follow to get the full benefits of anti-ageing:

1. Minerals

Yes! Minerals play an important part in keeping your body healthy and young. The body needs essential minerals for proper fluid balance, nerve transmission, muscle health, healthy bones, healthy teeth, brain functions and other so on. Minerals are also important for making enzymes and hormones. Essential minerals are of two kinds, namely, macro and micro minerals. Macro minerals include major minerals such as calcium, sodium, potassium, magnesium and phosphorus, among others. Micro minerals are the trace minerals such as iron, zinc, selenium, iodine and copper, among others.

2. Iron

Iron carries oxygen to our body and plays an important part in energy metabolism. An iron deficiency makes your nails brittle, and they break easily. A low iron count also results in anaemia and has many side effects such as low energy levels, weakness, pale and dull skin and many more. It is therefore important to keep your iron levels high by eating diverse foods from various sources that are rich in iron and also iron supplements. Iron found in foods including spinach, oysters, and cashews make your skin glow by activating B vitamins. You can find iron in organ meats, red meats, fish, poultry, shellfish (especially clams), egg yolks, legumes, dried fruits, dark and leafy greens and fortified cereals.

3. Zinc

These days everyone is aware of this powerful natural mineral and how it is required by the body for several functions. It is found in cells throughout the body and is necessary for immune functions and warding off bacteria and viruses. Zinc also helps in synthesising DNA and forming proteins. It is a natural anti-inflammatory agent and has been used to treat and prevent diarrhoea and the common cold. It is also known to boost male fertility, learning abilities and memory. Several studies have proved that zinc supplements can help in preventing hair loss. You can up your zinc levels by including in your diet foods such as oysters, pumpkin seeds, lentils, beef, coconut, spirulina and spinach. You could also check with your doctor and take a high-quality zinc supplement.

4. Selenium

Another very important mineral but needed only in small amounts is selenium. It is essential for good and glowing skin as it contains strong antioxidant properties. These properties help fight against cell damage caused by free radicals and slows down the signs of ageing, such as wrinkles, blemishes and skin spots, fine lines and skin dryness. In fact, research has shown that selenium offers a triple bonanza in that it not only protects against UV cell damage and skin inflammation but also protects against skin pigmentation. The recent research and studies continue to highlight the importance of selenium and other antioxidants for skin health and reducing the risk of skin cancer. A good dose of around 55 µg of selenium helps maintain healthy skin texture and colour. You can get selenium from dietary supplements or from foods such as Brazil nuts, liver, tuna, mushrooms, beans and seafood.

5. Coenzyme Q10

You might have not heard of this mineral, but it is definitely very important for your body. Coenzyme Q10 (CoQ10) is a fat-soluble vitamin (quinone) and a powerful antioxidant (its chemical constituent structure is similar to that of vitamin E). Due to its high antioxidant effects and preservative function, it is often added to creams and lotions. It helps counteract the skin cell damage caused by free radicals and helps preserve collagen and elastin stores. As a result, CoQ10 nurtures smoother, firmer and younger-looking skin. Although this is a naturally occurring compound in the body, its levels tend to decrease with age. Here's the big thing: it is one of the main factors that cause the skin to become wrinkled and saggy. Therefore, it is recommended that you take a daily dose of CoQ10 either through supplements or in your diet on a daily basis to protect your skin against the effects of ageing. Foods containing CoQ10 are peanuts, sardines, beef and organ meats from dietary supplements. CoQ10 is also used in many products as a fortifying compound.

6. Vitamin C with collagen

Do you have a glass of orange/amla/lemon juice every morning? Do you add bell peppers to your salad at lunch? If you did, your skin would be thanking you for not only being on a healthy diet but also ensuring that vitamin C is a part of it. Your body requires several nutrients to look and function its best, and vitamin C is an important player as it offers much more than just immunity-boosting properties. It contributes largely in helping rejuvenate your skin and protect your complexion whether you get it from food or apply it topically.

Vitamin C also plays a vital role in collagen production. Topical vitamin C encourages collagen production by stimulating fibroblasts (the same way eating broccoli and strawberries does), which reduce the appearance of fine lines. It also helps slow the synthesis of collagen while preserving the skin's structure. Various experiments have shown the effects of using vitamin C externally. This micronutrient is a powerful antioxidant and is used for preventing the effects of ageing and for treating hyperpigmentation. Adequate amount of vitamin C keeps the skin firm and strong while also aiding a faster recovery from wounds and cuts.

Research has also found that this important vitamin reduces the appearance of brown spots and other types of sun damage. It does this by protecting the skin against the harmful effects of free radicals. Other positive effects of this micronutrient on the skin include the reduction of inflammation and irritation, which means that you eventually have lesser red spots and blemishes. Simply put, vitamin C should be part of your skincare regimen—it is as important as washing your face or applying sunscreen.

How does vitamin C manage to do all this?

Vitamin C in action is almost like an army protecting its territory by neutralising free radicals before they wreak havoc and reducing inflammation. Research has also proved that women with the maximum intake of vitamin C have lesser noticeable wrinkles and dry patches on their skin. Vitamin C plays an important role in activating cells called fibroblasts that produce new collagen. This in turn improves the firmness and strength of the skin.

Vitamin C also works well when applied topically. It works wonders on the skin to fight free radical damage. It is important to use a product that has the L-ascorbic acid form of vitamin C—this actually penetrates to the deeper layers of your skin.

Rubbing vitamin C on the skin also counteracts the harmful effects of the UV rays that escape a sunblock lotion.

The recommended daily intake of vitamin C for men is 90 mg while for women it is 75 mg. Green peppers, broccoli, oranges (and orange juice), papaya, strawberries and cantaloupe are all excellent sources of vitamin C. Always keep in mind that when you want to choose a vitamin C skincare product, search the ingredient list for L-ascorbic acid.

7. Vitamin D

In recent years, there has been a widespread search for the 'fountain of youth', a product that would reverse tissue ageing. Research indicates that vitamin D has powerful anti-ageing properties and is known to significantly ward off wrinkles and protect against environmental aggressors including solar UV radiation by promoting skin cell turnover. In addition to being a stress-blocking vitamin that protects your heart, it has the ability to reverse ageing and ensure that you feel healthier and look younger.

What is Vitamin D?

Vitamin D is a fat-soluble vitamin that mainly supports calcium absorption, promoting growth and mineralisation of your bones. It is also necessary for the various functions of your immune, digestive, circulatory and nervous systems.

As we all know, vitamin D helps the body in absorbing calcium, which is critical to bone health and strength. Symptoms of a vitamin D deficiency could include muscle weakness, pain, fatigue and depression. To get enough D, look to certain foods, supplements and carefully planned sunlight exposure.

Foods that provide vitamin D include fatty fish, such as tuna, mackerel and salmon, orange juice, soy milk, cereals, beef liver, egg yolk and mushrooms.

8. Methylsulfonylmethane

Many people feel good when they look good as this instils confidence. We find that a lot of people place having healthy, vibrant skin at the top of their wish list. Here, Methylsulfonylmethane (MSM) can work to their advantage. MSM is a rich source of sulphur, which plays a major role in helping the body to produce collagen. Collagen is an essential ingredient in tissues that provides structural support to the skin while holding the human body together. Sulphur is also a building block of keratin, the chief structural constituent of hair and nails. Keratin is essential for strengthening the hair and influencing hair growth.

Sulphur is found in plants, animals and humans but can also be produced in a laboratory to create dietary supplements in powder or capsule form. Researchers have found that MSM helps normalise key genes responsible for healthy and young-looking skin. MSM also reduces the appearance of crow's feet and improves skin firmness. A clinical trial reported that 100% of the participants taking MSM showed a decrease in the number of wrinkles, with an average reduction of 38%. Additionally, the study reported improvements in skin elasticity and firmness.

The skin is a complex entity comprising of several layers. The topical and oral use of MSM ensures support from the outside while strengthening the internal processes that lead to long-term benefits.

MSM help boosts your immune system by reducing inflammation and increasing glutathione levels. It also helps reduce pain, muscle damage and oxidative stress after intense exercise, helping you recover more quickly and thereby improving your quality of life.

Some rich sources of MSM include coffee, beer, tomatoes, alfalfa sprouts, leafy green vegetables, apples, raspberries and also whole grains. Typical adult dosages range from 500 to 8,000 mg and MSM supplements may be taken daily with or after meals.

9. Pau d'arco tea

Pau d'arco is a supplement derived from the inner bark of a tropical tree used in traditional medicine in Central and South America. I know this sounds like Latin to you, but believe me, it is true! The inner bark has been used to treat a wide range of ailments and is known to reduce inflammation in the body. Several compounds called naphthoquinones, mainly lapachol and beta-lapachone, have been isolated from this inner bark and are thought responsible for its purported benefits. Its extract is also known to promote weight loss by inhibiting dietary fat absorption.

How do you make the tea?

Traditionally, 2–3 teaspoons (10–15 grams) of the bark is simmered in water for 15 minutes and consumed thrice per day.

10. Barley grass

Barley grass can be easily found at your favourite health stores and is frequently used in green juices and supplements alongside other greens such as kale, spinach and wheatgrass. Also known as barley leaves and barley greens, barley grass is the leaf of the barley plant. Extensive studies have been conducted to know its health benefits.

It is known as the new superfood and used often as a supplement to boost weight loss, enhance immune function and support overall health.

Barley grass comprises thousands of enzymes that help counteract the numerous carcinogens we are exposed to in daily modern life. Young sprouted barley leaves are one of the most abundant sources of superoxide dismutase (SOD), an anti-aging enzyme. Free radicals, unstable oxygen molecules that constantly bombard organs and tissues, are formed during routine activities such as breathing and eating. Increasing research on barley has found that barley grass juice is one of the best sources of SOD that can delay or even slow down the aging process, consequently lengthening the human life span. The body counters the negative effects of ageing through naturally produced antioxidants, such as SOD.

Barley grass is rich in a variety of important nutrients. Dried barley grass is a great source of fibre, containing approximately 3 gm per tablespoon (10 gm). Each serving of barley grass contains a high amount of vitamin A, a fat-soluble vitamin that regulates immune function, cell growth and vision. Barley also has a high amount vitamin C, which plays a central role in everything from skin health to wound healing to oral health.

Barley is also rich in essential micronutrients like vitamin K, which is needed for blood clotting, bone formation and heart health. Barley has a high composition of antioxidants that reduce oxidative stress and protect against chronic disease.

Barley grass also contains compounds such as saponarin, gamma-aminobutyric acid (GABA) and tryptophan, all of which have been linked to decreased blood pressure, reduced inflammation and improved heart health.

How to juice barley grass:

1. Take barley grass in a blender and add enough water to allow the grass to liquefy.
2. Blend the barley grass and water just long enough for the grass to dissolve.
3. Pour the mixture through a clean tight-weave towel or fine-mesh strainer into a clean glass or bowl.
4. Squeeze the liquid from the blended grass into the glass, making sure to get as much out as possible.
5. Discard the pulp and enjoy barley grass juice.
6. You can add this as a green in smoothies and salads.

I have been consuming a green smoothie every day for almost a decade! This can be quickly made and is a powerhouse of all vital vitamins and minerals. You can blend fresh fruits and dark greens together to whip up a quick and healthy meal that will transform your body inside out.

Smoothies are originally made with fruit and water (or a dairy base), which is high in sugar and can cause inflammation. A green smoothie is made with fruit, water (or a plant-based liquid) and leafy greens. A green smoothie can taste just as good as a regular smoothie but has many more health benefits.

You can use all types of greens from spinach and kale to chard and bok choy. Including leafy greens in your smoothie adds extra phytonutrients and fibre, which slows down the absorption of sugars into your body. One of my favourite greens is baby spinach because it is mild in taste and allows all the fruit's taste to come through. It is also easy to find all year round and affordable.

How do you make a green smoothie?

1. Select your basic ingredients. You can start with a leafy green such as spinach, kale, collard greens or lettuce. Lettuce is the mildest, while kale has the most pronounced flavour.
2. Pick a liquid such as almond milk, coconut water or even regular water. Milk will give the smoothie a milkshake-like consistency, while water will give it more of a juice-like consistency.
3. Pick some fruit to balance out the flavour of the leafy greens. For a green smoothie, you could use pineapple, banana, mango, pear, kiwi, avocado, green apples, a combination of these or other yellow and green fruits.
4. You can add some more flavour, more sweetness or even more nutritional value with all kinds of seeds, protein powders, natural sweeteners, nuts or nut butters, oils or spices.
5. Put it all in a blender and blend until it attains a smooth consistency with no chunks of leafy greens or fruits.

A smoothie for glowing skin:

To get glowing skin, you must make a smoothie that contains spinach, avocado and almond milk. They have amazing benefits and are especially great for your skin. Spinach has high levels of folic acid, which helps repair DNA and is great for renewing your skin. Avocado is full of monounsaturated fatty acids, which are actually good fats that help keep your skin moist and hydrated. Almond milk is loaded with vitamin E which is great for repairing your skin and defending against sun damage.

11. Green salads

We sometimes stick to the same boring cucumber, tomato, capsicum and onion salads and eventually lose interest in eating salads altogether. But green salads provide very high nutritional value and should be consumed daily. You could shake things up and give your leafy meals a healthy skin boost with some good-for-you ingredients.

Salads are very easy to make, including the dressing—which is a must in our busy lives. I can prepare a salad in under 5 minutes. Yes, even a homemade dressing can be made simply with a combination of lemon and olive oil.

Salads are an easy option if you want to include your daily veggies in your diet while keeping your calorie count down. You need to carefully choose your toppings and the dressing to keep out excess calories and unhealthy fat. Salad greens are a great source of vitamins, especially A, C and K. Many are high in iron, and some even have surprising amounts of calcium. Add that to the fact that many of them contain disease-fighting phytonutrients and it is hard to find a reason not to go for leafy greens whenever you can.

How do you choose the best salad greens?

You can easily tell fresh greens from those that are past their prime. Salad greens should be vibrant and crisp—avoid those showing signs of wilting, yellowing or brown spots. Head varieties should be tightly furled, not loose or limp.

Why should you eat salad greens?

They're incredibly good for you! As a general rule, the darker the green, the more nutrient-dense it is. Dark greens such as kale and spinach contain huge amounts of vitamins such as A, C, iron and calcium—and have found their rightful place on all superfood lists. On the other hand, paler greens such as iceberg lettuce are lower on the nutritional scale but have a low calorie count and high fibre and are generally very hydrating.

What are some great green leafy veggies for your salads and how are they beneficial?

Kale supports the detoxification enzymes in the liver and aids the general functions of the liver and kidney, which are the main detox organs of the body. Kale is also rich in magnesium, which helps relax muscles, relieving tension and aiding sleep and digestion.

Watercress and spinach are rich in iron, vital for preventing fatigue. Iron is also needed for transporting oxygen in the blood around the body, including to the skin and also provides magnesium for energy production.

12. Probiotics

The word 'probiotics' literally means 'for life'. Probiotics play a very important role in slowing down ageing. Multiple studies have found that probiotics can restore the pH of acidic skin, reduce the impact of oxidative stress, decrease the effects of photo-ageing, boost skin barrier function and improve the quality of your hair.

What are probiotics?

Probiotics are live bacteria and yeasts that are good for your digestive system. Our body is full of both good and bad bacteria. Probiotics are classified under 'good bacteria' because they help keep your gut healthy.

Probiotics are known for their various health benefits, especially in regulating gut health and strengthening the immune system. Recent studies have emphasized the role of probiotics and probiotic-containing fermented products in cosmetics and ageing.

Ageing is closely associated with a diversity of gut microbiota that are related to the changes in the gastrointestinal tract, and in dietary patterns, together with an associated decline in cognitive and immune function, eventually contributing to infirmity. Lactic acid bacteria are known for their ability to extend the lifespan and/or good health.

Types of probiotics

There are several classified under 'probiotics' that have different benefits, but most come from the following groups:

Lactobacillus
It is the most common form of probiotics and is found in yogurt and other fermented foods. It helps people who can't digest lactose, the sugar component in milk.

Bifidobacterium
It helps ease IBS and many other conditions. It can be found in fermented foods such as yogurt, kimchi, olives, sauerkraut, salami and kombucha.

Saccharomyces boulardii
This is a yeast found in probiotics and helps fight digestive problems. Food sources of Saccharomyces boulardii include yogurt, kefir, sauerkraut, kombucha, kimchi and miso, which are all rich with digestion-supporting probiotics. When consumed daily, they promote the growth of the natural flora in your digestive tract and support overall health.

13. Colostrum
This is a nutrient-rich fluid that is produced by female mammals immediately after giving birth. It is a complex biological fluid loaded with immunity, growth and tissue-repair properties. It is very nutritious and contains high levels of antibodies, which are proteins that fight infections and bacteria. Several research studies have proven that colostrum supplements are effective in boosting immunity in adults.

Colostrum promotes growth and good health in infants and new-born animals, but research shows that taking bovine colostrum supplements may promote immunity, help fight infections and improve gut health throughout life.

While colostrum is rich in macronutrients, vitamins and minerals, it has health benefits that are mostly linked to specific protein compounds, which include the following:

Lactoferrin

It is a protein enhancing your body's immune response to infections, including those caused by bacteria and viruses.

Bovine colostrum

It is high in two protein-based hormones, insulin-like growth factors 1 and 2 or IGF-1 and IGF-2.

Immunoglobulins

These are antibodies or proteins employed by your immune system to fight bacteria and viruses.

14. Detox

'You are what you eat.'

For starters, detoxification removes all the toxins from your body that actually speed up ageing. Toxics cause oxidation, which makes you age faster. Detoxing helps reduce the oxidation effect and allows your cells to function more efficiently.

What is a body detox?

A body detox is the process of removing toxins from the body. It also alludes to living in a way that keeps you young and helps maintain your energy levels. Detoxing also makes you look and feel younger. Removing toxic chemicals from your system makes your tissues healthier, improves blood flow, increases oxygen levels, improves skin and hair health and improves your mood. This combination makes you younger from the inside out. There are several methods of detoxing.

What is an anti-ageing detox?

An anti-ageing detox is one that focuses completely on removing the toxins that speed up the body's biological and visual ageing process. Removing these toxins makes you look and feel younger.

Can detoxing also happen naturally?

Yes, some organs in your body are specifically designed for removing toxins, such as your liver. The rate at which your body can remove toxins varies from person to person, and in most people, there is a build-up of toxins. The unhealthier your lifestyle, the more toxins your body will contain. As a result, regular manual detoxes are the best course of action.

Why is it important to detox?

Detox drinks have gained immense recognition in the fitness world for preventing toxic overload and averting major health problems. By detoxing your body, you help the vital organs of your body cleanse themselves of the toxins and enable the liver to function properly to excrete them.

The healthier you eat, the fewer harmful chemicals, fats, toxins and other non-nutritional elements there are in your system. There are a two things that you should remember when considering this. First, you should eat a healthy diet. This will help your body in a range of ways, including keeping it free from toxins and making you look and feel younger. Second, toxins can form in your body through methods other than the food you consume. Toxins can build up because of stress or hormonal imbalances. There are also toxins in the air that you breathe on a daily basis.

When should you detox?

Your body will show you signs that will tell you when you need to detox. You would probably feel the need even more intensely after a period of over-indulgence and inadequate exercise. The best example of this is the holiday season. In fact, this is often why people choose health-related goals as their New Year's resolutions.

The most important thing to remember, however, is to listen to your body. It will give you signs that you may need to detox. These include having irritated skin despite your usual skin-care routine. You might also feel bloated for unknown reasons, or you might be regularly fatigued. Puffy eyes and general sluggishness and are all signs too.

How does detoxing help you look and feel younger?

For a start, detoxing removes the toxins in your body that speed up ageing. Additionally, high toxin levels cause oxidation and damage your cells, thereby making you age faster. Detoxing reduces the oxidation effect and allows your cells to function more efficiently, decelerating the ageing process.

Detoxing also cleanses your pores, keeping your skin fresh and vibrant looking. Detoxing can help get rid of acne as well as make your hair and nails healthier.

It also boosts your immune system and increases your energy levels, which in itself makes you look and feel younger. This also keeps you active, which further promotes anti-ageing.

Some detox programmes

Colon cleanse

Colon cleanse is a process in which large quantities of water, up to 16gal (about 60l), and possibly other substances such as herbs or coffee, are flushed through the colon. This is done using a tube that's inserted into the rectum.

Other natural ways include the following:

Water flush

Drinking plenty of water, up to 6–8 glasses of lukewarm water each day, and staying well hydrated is a great way to regulate digestion and detox your body. You can also eat fruits and vegetables that have high water content like watermelons, tomatoes, lettuce and celery.

Saltwater flush

Saltwater flushing of the colon helps people experiencing severe constipation and irregularity in bowel movements. Before you eat anything in the morning, mix two teaspoons of sea salt or Himalayan salt with lukewarm water. Drink this water on an empty stomach to get full benefits, and in some time, you'll probably feel an urge to go to the bathroom.

High-fibre diet
High fibre content can be found in whole, healthy plant foods such as fruits, vegetables, grains, nuts, seeds and more. These contain cellulose and fibres that help 'bulk' up the excess matter in the colon. They also relieve constipation and regulate overactive bowels, while boosting helpful bacteria as a probiotic. They also foster gut bacteria.

Juices and smoothies
Fruit and vegetable juices are popular colon cleansers. You can practise fruit and vegetable juice fasts and cleanses, which are known as master cleanses.

15. Probiotics
Adding probiotics to the diet is another way to cleanse the colon since it also boosts the overall health in many other ways. You can include probiotic-rich foods such as yogurt, kimchi, pickles and other fermented foods in your diet. This helps introduce good bacteria to the gut with the help of fibre and resistant starches. These avert inflammations and promote regularity in bowel movements, which is very important for digestive health. ACV is a good probiotic and can be used as a colon cleanser.

16. Herbal teas
Herbal teas are also a great way to ensure digestive health. Laxative herbs such as psyllium, aloe vera, marshmallow root and slippery elm help with constipation.

Other herbs such as ginger, garlic and cayenne pepper contain antimicrobial phytochemicals that help suppress bad bacteria. They're therefore included in lots of cleanses, though more research about them is needed. Have one cup of these herbal teas a day.

17. Epsom salt detox
Detox baths are now gaining popularity and go beyond just soothing and boosting your overall well-being by strengthening the immune system and preventing disease. An Epsom salt detox entails a nice warm bath with Epsom salt that helps improve the body's natural detoxification process and promotes healing. The two main ingredients of Epsom salt are magnesium and sulphate. Magnesium is a natural substance that aids a variety of bodily functions, including the removal of toxins. Sulphate can strengthen the walls of the digestive tract and make it easier to release toxins. It is believed the combination of both these ingredients stimulates detoxification pathways.

Here are some benefits of the Epsom salt detox:

Soothes the skin
It helps soften rough, dry skin and exfoliate dead skin cells.

Reduces redness, soreness and pain
It provides pain relief and reduces swelling in people with inflammatory conditions such as rheumatoid arthritis, lupus, gout and psoriatic arthritis.

Reduces stress
A good magnesium level can boost brain neurotransmitters that help induce sleep and reduce stress. Magnesium may also stimulate melatonin, a sleep-inducing hormone.

How do you take an Epsom salt detox bath?

Only use Epsom salt that has been tested and approved for human use and has a standard mark on it. The packaging of the Epsom salt must have the details of the ingredients and drug fact information printed on it. Always purchase Epsom salt from a trusted medical or grocery shop.

To take an Epsom salt bath, add two cups of Epsom salt to a standard-sized bathtub. The salt will quickly dissolve under running water. The water should be warm and of a temperature between 33°C and 37°C. Soak yourself in the bathtub for 12–20 minutes, or longer if desired, and avoid using soap. You should rest for at least one hour after a detox bath or take the bath at bedtime so that you can go to sleep afterwards.

Other ingredients that can be added to an Epsom salt bath to enhance its effects include the following:

Olive oil
Olive oil contains antioxidants and can also help soften the skin when added to bathwater. You can add half a cup of olive oil as the bathtub is filling up with water.

Essential oils
Therapeutic oils can make a detox bath more relaxing. Some oils you can try include:

- Lavender oil
- Vanilla oil
- Bergamot oil

- Frankincense oil
- Eucalyptus oil

Essential oils need to be diluted before application, and so it is best to dilute them in a carrier oil before bathing. Add 3–5 drops of the essential oil per half to one ounce of carrier oil.

18. Baking soda
Baking soda has been shown to have antifungal properties, and it inhibits germ growth. It may also soften the skin and reduce itchiness.

19. Exercise
According to an article recently posted on *Inverse*, 'As people age, they lose muscle mass and the risk of heart disease, dementia and reduced immune function increases. As the years tick by, it becomes harder for people to bounce back from a workout injury or illness'.

What can be done to slow down or reverse these ageing effects?

For years, researchers have encouraged exercise for 'promoting health span and giving people extra disease-free years' and ultimately 'slowing down the degenerative process'. However, according to new research, experts have found that consistent aerobic exercise may not only slow down the effects of ageing but ultimately even 'reverse' them.

After conducting many experiments and studies on the effects of exercise on anti-ageing, scientists discovered that this 'exercise effect on muscle stem cells and tissue repair comes down to a tiny protein called cyclin D1'. Aerobic exercise has a way of 'restoring these cyclin D1 levels in dormant stem cells back to youthful levels, effectively accelerating muscle stem cell regeneration'.

Inverse explained that 'if the research translates to humans, it means jogging, swimming, cycling and other aerobic activities can help older people recover as quickly and efficiently as their younger selves. In the far future, these results could inform the creation of a drug that de-ages muscle stem cells'.

Improving the quality of life

Exercise not only prevents the onset of many diseases but also helps cure or alleviate others, improving the overall quality of your life. Recent studies of recreational cyclists aged 55–79 years suggest they have the capacity to do their daily tasks easily and efficiently because nearly all parts of their body are in a remarkably good condition.

The cyclists also scored highly on tests measuring the mental agility, mental health and quality of life.

Modern problems

In today's world, we have mostly been able to escape from problems arising from our sedentary lifestyle by leaning on the crutches of modern medicine. But while our average life expectancy has increased quite rapidly, our 'health span'—the period of life where we are free from disease—has not.

Keep your brain strong

The average brain shrinks by approximately 5 per cent every decade after the age of forty, but aerobic exercise significantly helps in maintaining the volume. 'When you exercise you produce a chemical called brain-derived neurotrophic factor (BDNF), which may help to prevent age-related decline by reducing the deterioration of the brain,' says Joseph Firt, the author of a study on the subject. In this study, exercise included stationary cycling, walking and running on a treadmill 2–5 times a week for 3–24 months. Along with regulating regular healthy ageing, exercise prevents ageing-related neurodegenerative disorders such as Alzheimer's and dementia.

- As we age, there are many forms of aerobic exercise that are the most important to fight the effects of ageing. Aerobic exercises such as jogging may help reverse some heart damage from normal ageing.
- Strength training moves such as tai chi are best for protecting the muscles from age-related decline.
- There is a significant link between regular cardio exercises such as swimming and walking and a lower risk of dementia.
- Activities such as cycling may protect your immune system from age-related decline.
- Meditation helps bring in calm and peace and yoga helps keep your body flexible. It also brings in that natural glow.

Lastly, here are some good anti-ageing foods to eat. These will help with your anti-ageing detox:

- Fresh fish, particularly salmon, sardines and other fish that have high levels of omega-3 fatty acids. The essential vitamins in fish also help with the detox process.
- Red peppers, because they contain high amounts of vitamin C, carotene and the anti-ageing detox folate.
- Herbal tea; the herbs give your body an antioxidant boost, helping to remove harmful toxins.
- Leafy green vegetables, particularly broccoli and spinach. They are high in vitamins and minerals, including iron.

Always remember that good health starts from within. Don't stress yourself trying to do things that you are not comfortable with. Try out new things to stay youthful but in a week or so check if you are comfortable following them. I have given many options and substitutes that you can experiment with. Do what suits your body. And above all, stay happy and calm always.

13

The Lifestyle Detox Diet

---•---

DETOXIFICATION, OR DETOX, is the removal of toxins from the body. If I get into the details of detox, I will have to write another book. But for now, we are going to look at the lifestyle approach towards detoxification. Do you think you can detox every day? When do you need to detox the most? And how exactly do you do it?

In this chapter, we will look into a daily as well as a monthly detox routine. You can also practice the latter after a weekend or a vacation of junk eating.

Your body, especially your gut, which is your main line of defence, accumulates a lot of toxins that come from processed or undigested foods, alcohol, sugary foods and so on. Both the good and the bad bacteria are formed to keep your body healthy, but as soon as the percentage of toxins and bad bacteria rises, they start percolating into your bloodstream, causing inflammation in your entire body. This also leads to a lot of lifestyle and other diseases since it weakens your immune system. This is the main reason we are going to talk about gut detoxification in this chapter.

DAILY GUT DETOX

Yes, that's correct. There are some lifestyle habits that help you detoxify on a day-to-day basis. Here are some options:

1. Have lukewarm water with a pinch of turmeric and half a lemon every morning on an empty stomach.
2. Have raw unfiltered ACV with water at room temperature with some turmeric .
3. Have neem juice or capsules (500 mg) on an empty stomach along with your morning drink.
4. Have celery juice with lemon, sea salt and black pepper every day at around 4:00 p.m.
5. Follow intermittent fasting at least five days a week.
6. Take probiotic-rich foods or supplements daily.

These are some basic and simple practices that you can follow every single day of your life and you will soon notice the wonders they do to your health and fitness.

MONTHLY DETOX

Now let's talk about a proper detox diet routine that you should ideally practice once every month, when you are starting to get on a healthy eating journey, when you are just back from a vacation or when you know you have eaten unhealthy and are feeling very bloated and lethargic and have tremendous acne breakout or hair fall.

Detox Diet (basic)

Immediately after waking up: 1 glass water (room temp) with 1 tsp raw unfiltered ACV
Breakfast: lemon/ginger/tulsi tea, 1–2 moong dal chilla + 5 almonds + 5 walnuts
Mid-morning snack: 1 glass (carrots + orange) juice with sabza seeds (basil seeds)
Lunch: vegetable salad with mushrooms + homemade buttermilk (2 glasses)
Mid-afternoon snack: curd (homemade) + 1 bowl mixed seeds + 5 pistachios
Dinner: 1–2 bowls cooked sprouts with lots of added vegetables
Before sleeping: 1 glass water (room temp) with 1 tsp raw unfiltered ACV

CASE STUDY 3	
Client profile	• Age: 29 years • Weight: 71.2 kg • Height: 5 ft. 2 in.
Medical complications	• Poly-cystic ovarian disease

\multicolumn{2}{c}{**CASE STUDY 3**}
Other complaints	- Hair fall
- Acne
- Chronic constipation
- Obesity
- Low self-esteem
Existing diet and exercise routine	- Junk food
- No exercise
- Late-night binge watching
Diet changes recommended	- Gut cleansing—detox teas, triphala tablets (for 7 days)
- Probiotics to balance hormones and purify blood
- Fibrous foods
- Intermittent fasting
Exercise routine recommended	- HIIT and weight training
Other recommendations	- None
Improvement in condition	- Weight loss: 3 kg after a week of detox and then 10 kg to 61.4
- PCOD completely resolved
- Acne cleared

14

The Lifestyle Nutrition Kitchen

---·---

(This chapter contains simple replacements in the kitchen that will make sure that the food you prepare is healthy too!)

I CAME UP with the lifestyle kitchen design because I believe that healthy food comes from a healthy kitchen equipped with the right ingredients. It is very important that you use the right ingredients in cooking. Moreover, if your kitchen is stocked up with the right foods, you can reach out to them during those moments of cravings or hunger. I am enlisting the most basic and important ingredients of a healthy kitchen below. So before starting on the lifestyle diet plan, make sure you have your lifestyle nutrition kitchen all set up!

1. Salt: rock salt, sea salt, black salt, pink salt
2. Sugar: stevia (the green powder of stevia and not the processed drops), raw organic jaggery, raw manuka honey, raw organic honey
3. Flour (atta): home-ground atta; mix all grains with some amounts of different dals when you make your atta. You can also make flour with any of the following wholegrains or millets: quinoa, rajgira (amaranth), jowar, bajra, nachni, rala (fox millet), khapali gehu (organic wheat with fibre)
4. Fats and oils: desi ghee (cow ghee), cold-pressed coconut oil, groundnut oil, black sesame oil, avocado oil (all ghani or cold-pressed oils)
5. Legumes and dals: moong dal, black bean, chawli, chole, soya, tur dal and the like. If you have digestive issues with any dal or legume, all you have to do is soak or sprout them.
6. Rice: brown rice, red rice (soak or sprout before cooking)
7. Indian spices: all Indian herbs and spices
8. Cinnamon powder: use for coffees and teas. This is an excellent fat burner.
9. Nuts: almonds, walnuts, cashew, pistachio, hazelnuts, dried figs and dates (all nuts)
10. Seeds: pumpkin, sunflower, chia, flax, hemp, basil, watermelon
11. Chocolate: dark chocolate (80% min)
12. Vegetables: all seasonal
13. Fruits: all seasonal
14. Drinks: coffee (no sugar and milk), green tea, herbal tea, homemade ginger tea, matcha green tea and all other teas

15. Raw unfiltered apple cider vinegar (ACV) is a must-have in all the kitchens
16. Greens and chlorophyll boost: all green leafy vegetables, wheatgrass, spirulina
17. Milk: almond milk, coconut milk, nut milk
18. Fermented foods: curds, kefir, kombucha, kimchi, sauerkraut, pickles

Stock up on these and watch your family's health transform!

15

How to Choose Smartly between Carbohydrates, Proteins and Fats

COMPLEX CARBOHYDRATES

BREAKFAST IS THE first meal of the day, and some good healthy complex carbohydrates are one of the most important components of a healthy breakfast. The body burns complex carbohydrates slowly throughout the day, making sure your blood sugar levels are stable. The foods that fall into this category are whole grains, brown rice, vegetables (especially peas and beans), millets, ragi, jowar, bajra, buckwheat (kuttu) and rajgira (amaranth).

What are complex carbohydrates?

Complex carbohydrates are the carbohydrates that in their natural food form are comprised of a long chain of simple carbohydrates (three or more) linked together. They are a good blend of healthy sugars, vitamins, minerals, and lots of fibre that helps prevent a sugar spike in your bloodstream.

Why is it important to have complex carbohydrates instead of simple carbohydrates?

- They help maintain good energy levels throughout the day. Carbohydrates provide the body with immediate energy. Denying yourself will only leave you feeling low on energy the entire day. When you consume complex carbohydrates in the morning for breakfast, your body burns them throughout the day without any fatigue. So you never suffer the 'thud' that you would with caffeine or sugar.
- They help maintain steady blood sugar levels.
  This point is specifically for people with diabetes. Complex carbohydrates are one of the best foods for everyone suffering from this condition. They have a much lower glycaemic index than most simple carbohydrates. They keep your sugar levels stable, thus preventing cravings as well.
- They help in digestion.
  Healthy complex carbohydrates contain fibre, which helps in good digestion.
- They keep the body's metabolism rate high.

Complex carbohydrates help your body release energy steadily throughout the day, thus keeping your metabolism rate high. Without these calories that also give you energy, your body and its metabolism would suffer the most.

- They help you get a good sleep.

   Certain carbohydrates like sweet potatoes, rice and red pumpkin contain vast quantities of tryptophan and melatonin. This relaxes your body and mind, aiding you in sleeping well.

- They balance the nervous system.

   While simple and refined sugar makes you jittery and anxious, complex carbohydrates produce a calming effect on the body, thus reducing nervousness and anxiety. That is why you often feel less stressed after having a banana or some roasted sweet potatoes. Good carbohydrates help your body produce several enzymatic reactions and bring balance in just about every way possible.

- They improves brain functions.

   Your body uses carbohydrates for ideal brain functioning. Foods such as different vegetables, quinoa, beans, legumes, nuts, seeds and fruits contain an array of carbohydrates that help establish mental focus and maintain a healthy mood. Without carbohydrates, you may feel light-headed, have a hard time concentrating, feel sad or depressed or just not feel like yourself. You may also have a harder time remembering and recollecting information.

So do not deprive your body of carbohydrates; it needs them!

Here are the best ways to integrate carbs into your meals:

- Complex carbohydrates: Breakfast and lunch
- Simple carbohydrates (such as fruits): Mid-morning snack with some seed toppings.

    For your mid-morning snack, i.e. the snack between your breakfast and lunch, you should always have fresh fruits with any seeds toppings, e.g. pumpkin seeds, basil seeds, chia seeds, sunflower seeds and so on. When you top fruits with seeds, their glycaemic index is reduced, thereby preventing your blood sugar from spiking. This is highly beneficial for all diabetes patients.
- Complex carbohydrates only: Dinner (rice and vegetables)

PROTEINS

The simplest definition of proteins goes like this: 'they are the basic building blocks of the body'. That is why we need lots of proteins for the growth and maintenance of the body.

Best dietary protein options:

- Non-vegetarian: Eggs, chicken, fish, mutton (once in 15 days)
- Vegetarian: All nuts and seeds (most effective when consumed soaked in water), all beans and lentils, mushrooms, makhana, all types of dals

Health benefits of proteins:

1. They help you maintain and even lose weight.
2. They stabilise your blood-sugar levels.

3. They improve your ability to learn and concentrate.
4. They support the growth and maintenance of muscles.
5. They prevent premature ageing.
6. They tighten the skin naturally.
7. They help reduce hair fall.
8. They promote cell and tissue regeneration.
9. They enhance the functioning of most body enzymes.

When should you have proteins?

People always ask me this question. The answer is very simple and easy to adopt. You need to have proteins with literally every meal. For example, have some eggs with breakfast, dal with lunch, sprouts or chicken or fish with dinner, nuts and seeds or makhanas with snacks. Make sure that your every meal has some protein in it. The Indian diet is predominantly high in carbohydrates, and therefore our body naturally becomes protein deficient if we don't consciously watch our protein intake. So ensure you always include proteins in each meal.

Best meals in which to have proteins: Breakfast, lunch, dinner and snacks.

FATS ARE GOOD!

Over the last twenty or so years, people have stopped eating everything that has any fats in it. They stopped consuming coconuts, ghee, egg yolk, peanuts, and most nuts and seeds, convinced that these fatty foods will increase their cholesterol levels and invite heart diseases, hypertension or weight gain.

Hence low-fat or no-fat food products started coming in the market, and so did hormonal disorders such as polycystic ovary syndrome (PCOS) and thyroid. Also, the number of heart disease and hypertension patients has been increasing over the last two decades. This is a clear sign that we need to change our understanding of fats and know what good fats are and why we need them.

First of all, let us clear the cholesterol and heart diseases confusion. Well, there are two types of cholesterols in your body, good cholesterol (HDL) and bad cholesterol (LDL). The good cholesterol helps you balance your hormones and maintain the right weight and also protects you from cardiovascular diseases. Maintaining optimum levels of good cholesterol is necessary to have a healthy body. You get an abundance of good cholesterol as well as omega 3, 6 and 9 fatty acids and many more nutrients from foods such as avocado, coconuts, peanuts, almonds, ghee, coconut butter, egg yolk and all nuts and seeds. Bad cholesterol is the one that causes weight gain, hypertension, hormonal imbalances and many cardiovascular diseases. The foods leading to an increase in bad cholesterol include all processed foods, refined sugar, hydrogenated oils, fried foods, bread (gluten) in excessive quantities and dairy products.

Now that we have thrown some light on cholesterol and heart diseases, let us discuss good fats and their benefits.

My life changed entirely since I started having coffee with butter/ghee first thing in the morning. I started this ritual eight years back and haven't got off it since. It has helped me clear my skin, and my acne is completely under control. It has kept me away from any hormonal imbalances. It has made my hair thicker and shinier, and my face and skin have a nice glow now. It has also helped me lose weight faster by accelerating my body's fat-burning process and boosting my metabolism. I have discussed butter coffee in detail in the following chapters. So if you haven't tried the butter coffee ritual, then do get on it as soon as possible. If you are allergic to caffeine or do not like coffee, you can have butter tea (I have seen many people in Himachal Pradesh drink butter tea traditionally) or you can simply start your day with a type of healthy fat—handful soaked nuts or seeds or one tablespoon ghee/cold-pressed coconut oil with warm water or one avocado. This will immensely benefit your body and help your stabilise your blood sugar level in the morning, which is one of the most sensitive times for sugar spikes. So this ritual is the best for diabetics as well.

When you combine good fats with healthy carbohydrates in a food item, the glycaemic index of that food drops, making sure your blood sugar does not spike at all. Examples of such items include dal, rice and ghee, fresh fruits with mixed seeds on top and smoothies with coconut malai/almond milk/avocados/nuts, among others. These small modifications will make your food both super tasty and super healthy. They will also keep your blood sugar levels in check. So all the diabetics out there, don't be afraid of consuming good fats!

Health benefits of consuming good fats:

1. They help attain better body composition.
2. They aid weight loss.
3. They help achieve hormonal balance.

4. They help in the absorption of nutrients.
5. They promote a healthier digestive system.
6. They stabilise the body's blood sugar levels.
7. They boost the reproductive health.
8. They help achieve a better cholesterol ratio and reduce the risk of heart disease.
9. They promote skin and hair health.

When should you consume fats?

The best time to consume fats is in the morning immediately after your morning drink and on an empty stomach. You can also combine good fats with some proteins and veggies for a lighter and healthier dinner. You could also include avocados, nuts and seeds in your breakfast or snacks.

So, the best time to have good fats is early morning on an empty stomach, breakfast, dinner and snack time.

Now that we have discussed carbohydrates, proteins and fats from a novel point of view, let's look at an interesting and inspiring case study!

CASE STUDY 4	
Client profile	Age: 24 years
	Weight: 72.8 kg
	Height: 4 ft. 11 in.

CASE STUDY 4	
Body fat and blood analysis	BMI: 34.1 Overall fat: 34.5 Visceral fat: 19.5 Body age: 48 years Vitamin D deficiency Vitamin B12 deficiency
Requirement	Weight loss
Existing diet and exercise routine	Junk food Stress eating No exercise Late nights for studying
Diet changes recommended	Detox and gut cleansing—herbal teas, ACV, turmeric, etc. Alkaline foods Dairy- and gluten-free substitutes Collagen supplements Vitamin B12 supplements
Exercise routine recommended	Basic yoga Brisk walking
Other recommendations	Meditation Counselling Journaling
Improvement in condition	Weight loss from 72.8 kg to 67 kg in 3 months Increased strength and energy Reduced inches, as detailed below.

Body part	Before (inches)	After (inches)
Mid-arm	12	10
Mid-thigh	23	21
Upper abdomen	30	28
Lower abdomen	42	34.5
Middle abdomen	38	32
Chest	37	32.5

16

Food Cravings Are Real—Learn How to Deal with Them

'CRAVINGS' IS THE most commonly used word when it comes to following a healthy routine or getting on a diet. Do you know what causes cravings? Let's find that out first.

The main reason why you crave a certain food is because it contains a nutrient that is deficient in your body. For example, when there are long intervals between your meals, when you have starved for more than three hours or when you are on a low-carb or no-carb diet, your blood sugar levels drop significantly and you start craving high-sugar foods. It could be anything from sweets, pastries, bread, bakery products and so on.

Another example could be something that we see in kids: kids chronically eat bricks or soil particles when their body is iron deficient. If they are eating pencils or chalk, they could be calcium deficient. I have also seen many of my clients craving meat when their protein intake is much lesser than their body's daily requirement.

HERE IS A VERY SIMPLE APPROACH TO DEAL WITH CRAVINGS:

1. When you have cravings, pay very close attention to what kind of food you crave for. Also note if you crave a particular food at a specific time of the day.
2. Replace that food with a healthier option. You can satisfy your sweet cravings with healthy energy bars, naturally sweet foods such as dates or figs or healthy treats such as peanut or almond truffles. Meat cravings can be met with fresh and homemade chicken or fish.
3. Make sure you don't leave long intervals between your meals or snacks. Keeping filling in the gaps with small snacks or green juices or smoothies (have these every 3–4 hours).
4. When you are dehydrated, you tend to feel hungry or have certain cravings. So make sure you monitor your water intake.

Anti-craving superfoods

Here are two superfoods that will help you get rid of your cravings:

1. Nuts and seeds: All types of nuts and seeds help you stabilise your blood sugar levels and thus get rid of the cravings.

2. Butter coffee: In case you have a super-tight schedule and no time to eat nuts and seeds, just have a cup of butter coffee (please refer to the chapter on butter coffee). You can also have black coffee with one tablespoon of cold-pressed coconut oil if butter coffee is not possible to get.

Don't be scared of cravings or try to run away from them. You can now manage them in your way. With this approach, you can get over your cravings and be at peace too!

Foods that help you reduce cravings:

1. Dark chocolate (80% dark)
2. Chia seeds
3. Sabza seeds
4. Olive oil (add to your meals)
5. Ghee (add to your meals)
6. Black coffee
7. Green tea
8. High-protein vegan smoothies

Note: A diet rich in proteins and healthy fats always keeps your mind stable and reduces your cravings for unhealthy foods.

17

Lifestyle Habits and You

Do you want to have a healthier lifestyle? Wrong question? Who doesn't want to live a healthier life? You can start working towards it by making a few simple changes that lead to a sustained healthy lifestyle. Start by making a few simple changes to your day-to-day routine. Drastically trying to change habits will only bring you back to square one. Building these habits slowly over time will help you create a new lifestyle that you will be able to stick with in the long term.

HOW A DAILY ROUTINE CAN CHANGE YOUR LIFE

We can maintain a healthy lifestyle if we focus on daily routines. These daily routines structure your day and make the difference between operating at peak efficiency and struggling to make it through a poorly planned day. An excellent daily routine sets you up for success, and you feel more mindful and energised. The choice is yours. You can have energising and time-saving routines, or you can adopt draining and inefficient routines. The important thing is to recognise them so that you can make a change.

Are you motivated but unsure of where to start? Start with these five simple changes:

1. Morning meditation and pranayama

Meditation

An important habit I have formed over the last ten years is that of meditation. I have started meditating in the morning, which has helped me become more peaceful, more focused, less worried about discomfort and more appreciative and attentive to everything in my life. I am still far from perfect, but it has helped me come a long way.

Meditation has helped me understand my own mind. Before I started meditating, I never thought about what was going on inside my head. It would just happen, and I would follow its commands like an automaton. These days, all of that still happens, but I am more and more aware of what's going on. I can make a choice about whether to follow the commands.

I therefore recommend meditation early in the morning, just after waking up. While I am not saying it's easy, you can start small and get better and better as you practise. Don't expect to be good at first—that's why it's called 'practice'.

Here are some tips that can help you get started.

- Start with sitting quietly and meditating for just around 2 minutes. Do this once a day for a week. Once you feel comfortable with 2 minutes, increase the duration by another 2 minutes and do that for a week. If all goes well, by increasing just a little at a time, you'll be meditating for 10 minutes a day in the second month, which is very good. But start small.
- Meditate first thing every morning. We might decide to do it later in the day but tend to forget in the daily grind. Try setting an alarm to meditate every morning when you get up. You could also put a note that says 'meditate' somewhere where you are sure to see it.
- Don't get too worried about the posture and all the other minor things. You can start just by sitting on a chair, couch or even your bed. If you're comfortable on the ground, sit cross-legged. It is just going to be for 2 minutes at first anyway, so just sit. Later you can worry about adjusting your position so that you are comfortable for longer, but in the beginning it doesn't matter much. Just sit somewhere quiet and be comfortable.
- Check how your body feels and the quality of your thoughts. Busy? Tired? Anxious? See whatever you're bringing to this meditation session as being completely okay.
- Once you have settled into a comfortable position, start by counting your breaths. Just place the attention on your

breath as it comes in and follow it through your nose all the way down to your lungs. Try counting 'one' as you take in the first breath, then 'two' as you breathe out. Repeat this to the count of ten, then start again at one.

- At some point, your mind will begin to wander. This is almost certain. There's nothing wrong with that. When you feel your mind wandering, don't stress, but gradually return to your breath. Count 'one' again and start over. You might feel a little frustrated, but it's perfectly okay to not stay attentive; we all do it.
- When you notice thoughts and feelings arising during meditation, look at them calmly. Develop a loving attitude and see them as friends, not intruders or enemies. These feelings are all part of you, though not all of you.
- Don't worry about doing it wrong. That's okay too. There's no perfect way to do it, just be happy you're doing it.
- Don't get too stuck with thoughts of clearing the mind. People think that meditation is about clearing your mind or stopping all thoughts. It's not. This can sometimes happen, but it's not the 'goal' of meditation. Instead, just try to practise focusing your attention, and practise some more when your mind wanders.
- Focus on yourself. This practice isn't just about focusing your attention; it's about learning how your mind works. What's going on inside there? It's murky, but by watching your mind wander, get frustrated or avoid difficult feelings, you can start to understand yourself.
- Do a body scan. Another thing you can do, once you become a little better at following your breath, is focus your

attention on one body part at a time. Start by feeling the soles of your feet. Slowly move to your toes, the tops of your feet, your ankles, all the way to the top of your head.
- You can also focus on lights and sounds. Place your attention on the source of light around you. Just keep your eyes on one spot, and notice the light in the room you are in. On another day, just focus on noticing sounds. On yet another day, try to notice the energy in the room all around you (including light and sounds).
- You can practise meditation anywhere. If you're traveling and work comes up in the morning, you can meditate in your office. You can just sit in a park and you're done. You could also try meditation while commuting or as you walk somewhere. Sitting meditation is the best place to start, but in truth, you're practising for this kind of mindfulness in your entire life.

Find a community of people who meditate. Even better, find a community of people who meditate and join them. Or find an online group and check in with them and ask questions, get support and encourage others. Always smile when you're done and be grateful that you have this time to yourself. Be happy that you stuck with your commitment, that you showed yourself that you're trustworthy, that you took the time to get to know yourself and make friends with yourself. That's an amazing 2 minutes of your life. Meditation isn't always easy or even peaceful. But it has truly amazing benefits, and you can start today and continue for the rest of your life.

Pranayama

Pranayama is the control of one's breathing. Prana is the breath or vital energy in the body and represents the pranic energy responsible for life or life force, and 'ayama' means control.

One can control the rhythms of pranic energy with pranayama and develop a healthy body and mind. There are five types of prana that are responsible for various pranic activities in the body: prana, apana, vyan, udana and samana. The practice of pranayama achieves the balance in the activities of these forms of prana and results in a healthy body and mind.

Types of pranayama (taken from a Pranayam website to ensure that the right method is followed):

1. Natural breathing
Sit in a comfortable position with shoulders relaxed. Focus on your breathing and notice whether it is deep or shallow. Feel the temperature of your breath when air is inhaled and exhaled. Notice if there is any strain. Be aware only of the breath. Now try to become more aware of the breath entering the nostrils. Feel the breath flowing down towards the lungs. Follow the breath with the inhalation and exhalation. Try to focus only on the breath. Continue with this practice for as long as you feel comfortable.

2. Basic abdominal breathing
Make yourself comfortable and sit with pillows as a support behind your back or lie down at a 45 degree with pillows.

Place one hand on the belly and the other hand on the chest. Inhale deeply using the diaphragm and you will automatically see the diaphragm moving downward, pushing the abdomen down and out, making it rise. Upon exhalation, the diaphragm will move upward and the abdomen will fall. Continue the practice. If the chest is moving, then the breathing is still shallow, without using the diaphragm. If we use the diaphragm, then the lower lobes of the lungs are being used, improving their efficiency and having a positive effect on the heart, liver, stomach and intestines. It is the most natural and efficient way to breathe. However, many people do not breathe in this way due to their modern lifestyle. We can see huge benefits just by altering the way we breathe.

3. Thoracic breathing
This form of breathing is a stepping stone to bring in awareness on how we breathe and learn yogic breathing. This is the way many of us breathe usually. It expends more energy than abdominal breathing.

To practise thoracic breathing, one starts with breath awareness and then tries to focus on expanding the ribcage only, without using the diaphragm. The focus should be only on the expansion of the chest as one inhales and on the contraction of the chest as one exhales.

4. Clavicular breathing
Clavicular breathing is usually done along with thoracic breathing. This type of breathing brings down stress and also

treats airway obstruction. The upper ribs and collar bones are pulled upwards by the sternum and neck. This allows more air into the lungs. In yoga, we only use it only to create awareness and then combine it with thoracic and abdominal breathing for yogic breathing.

To practise this breathing, start with breath awareness and then thoracic breathing for a few minutes. After that breathe in fully, into the chest, and from there try to breathe in a little more so that you feel the expansion right into the upper lungs. The collar bones and shoulders will rise slightly. Exhale, first relaxing the neck and upper chest and then the ribcage.

5. Yogic breathing

This involves the use of the abdomen, chest and clavicular region. It can also be practised before other breathing techniques. It allows you to have maximum inhalation and exhalation and can be combined with deep breathing (using a ratio).

Inhale slowly, allowing the abdomen to rise. When the abdomen has expanded as much as it can, allow the chest to expand outwards and upwards. Once the ribs have expanded as much as they can, inhale a little more so that the collar bones move up slightly. Then slowly exhale, first allowing the collar bones to move downwards, then the chest and finally the abdomen. Continue the practice without any strain, jerks or tension. The breath should feel natural. After some time, it should be mostly thoracic and abdominal breathing. Abdominal breathing should be at least 70 per cent of the breathing.

6. Deep breathing

Start with breathing normally while keeping yourself aware of the abdomen and the chest. Inhale deeply and smoothly in counts (use a timer). Exhale smoothly in the required counts. Continue this process. Be aware of the abdomen rising and falling with the breath. Return to normal breathing. Practise another round if desired. Because the respiration rate drops, the heart rate reduces and blood pressure also comes down.

7. Fast breathing

There are various types of fast breathing exercises that we can follow. Use a combination of these:

- Inhale and exhale through both nostrils
- Close the right nostril and inhale and exhale through the left nostril
- Close the left nostril and inhale and exhale through the right nostril
- Inhale through the left nostril and exhale through the right nostril
- Inhale through the right nostril and exhale through the left nostril
- Inhale through the left nostril, exhale through the right, inhale through the right and then exhale through the left.

As you rapidly inhale and exhale, the carbon dioxide levels in the blood fall and oxygen levels rise. Rich oxygenated blood is supplied to the vital organs, improving their function. It helps in exchange of gases at a cellular level and removes toxins from the blood.

8. Viloma—interrupted breathing

In viloma breathing, you need to start with relaxed breathing. Imagine a set of stairs or a ladder in your body, with the base at the pelvic floor and the top at the throat.

Start inhaling, but instead of inhaling smoothly like in deep breathing, inhale in steps. Imagine you are walking up the steps or visualise the prana moving up the ladder in your body. There should be between three to five steps. Keep inhaling till you reach the top and the lungs are full. Slowly exhale, smoothly, without steps, till the lungs feel empty. Continue the practice.

9. Anulom vilom—alternate nostril breathing

Make the pranava mudra by bending the index and middle finger towards the palm. When we bring the right hand up to the nose, we can block the right nostril with the thumb and then change to blocking the left nostril with the ring finger, which may be supported with the little finger. In this way we can move the hand from side to side, as needed.

Slowly inhale through the left nostril, close the nostril and exhale slowly through the right nostril. Inhale through the right nostril and then exhale through the left nostril. This is one round. Continue at your own pace. Anulom vilom helps nourish the entire body with an extra supply of oxygen.

10. Cooling pranayamas—sheetali, sitkari and kaki mudra

Sheetali: Here you need to open your mouth and extend the tongue outside. Breathe through your mouth, then close the mouth and exhale through the nose. Make sure the breaths are slow, deep and comfortable.

Sitkari: Here you need to press your teeth together lightly. Separate the lips so that the teeth are exposed. Keep your tongue flat. Inhale slowly, through the teeth. Close the mouth and exhale slowly through the nose. Keep the breaths slow and relaxed.

Kaki mudra: Here you need to focus on the tip of your nose and purse your lips into the shape of a beak. Relax the tongue and inhale through the lips. Close the lips and exhale through the nose. Let the breath be slow and relaxed.

These pranayamas help in releasing the excess heat from the body, treating acidity, reducing blood pressure and also relaxing the muscles among many others.

11. Ujjayi—victorious breath

Here you need to focus on your throat and imagine that you are inhaling and exhaling through the throat. Contract the throat slightly on inhalation and exhalation. Keep the breath slow, relaxed and deep. Focus on the breath and sound. The sound should not be very loud and will be like a baby snoring. The breath will become slower as you continue. This helps lower high blood pressure, helps in natural relaxation and reduces heart problems and insomnia.

12. Bhramari—sounds like the humming bee

Inhale slowly and deeply through the nose. On exhalation, make the sound of 'm', as in the third letter of 'aum', or like the humming of a bee. Exhale slowly and do not strain. The exhalation will naturally be longer than the inhalation. If that is comfortable, block the ears with the fingers to increase the vibrations through the body. You can block your ears by placing your thumbs in them and having your elbows pointing out, arms by the sides of the head and fingers around the head. You can also block them with the index fingers, with the elbows pointing down and arms in front of the chest.

Bhramari pranayama helps strengthens the throat and voice muscles while also improving hearing. It also lowers blood pressure and heals the body tissues after surgery.

13. Bhastrika pranayama—lungs moving like bellows

Here you need to forcefully take deep breaths in and out through the nose. Do not strain. During inhalation, the abdomen moves outward as the diaphragm descends and is pulled in as one exhales. The movement should be slightly exaggerated but not in jerks. The speed should be gradually increased. Inhale through the right nostril slowly and then exhale through the left nostril. This is one round.

This pranayama has multiple benefits such as purifying blood, improving complexion, keeping the chest area and air passage clear, speeding up the metabolism of the body and reducing fat, removing excess mucus from the body and also helping balance the doshas.

14. Surya bhedan—right nostril breathing

As the name suggests, the name of this pranayama is a combination of 'surya' meaning sun and 'bheda' meaning to pierce/awaken. In the body, the pingala nadi represents the energy of the sun or vital energy. Surya bhedan therefore means to pierce or purify the pingala nadi. Here you need to inhale through the right nostril and exhale through the left nostril. This pranayama increases the vital energy of the body, stimulates the sympathetic nervous system and the left part of the brain, eliminating wind or gas related trouble (vata) and balancing acidity (pitta).

2. Gratitude journaling and prayer

This is a very important aspect of leading a fulfilling life. The word 'gratitude' is derived from the Latin word 'gratia', which means grace, graciousness or gratefulness (depending on the context). In a way, gratitude actually is a combination of all of these. Gratitude is a thankful appreciation for what an individual receives, whether tangible or intangible. With gratitude, people acknowledge the goodness in their lives. As a result, gratitude also helps people connect with something larger than themselves as individuals—whether to other people, nature or a higher power.

If we look at positive research that is backed by psychology, gratitude is strongly and constantly linked with greater happiness. It supports positive emotions in people, allows people to relish good experiences, improves their health, deals with adversity and builds strong relationships.

People feel and express gratitude in various ways. They can be thankful for elements of their childhood or past blessings, not take their good fortune for granted as it comes and maintain a hopeful and optimistic attitude. Regardless of the inherent or current level of someone's gratitude, it's a quality that individuals can successfully cultivate further.

Research on gratitude

Two psychologists, Dr Robert A. Emmons of the University of California, Davis, and Dr Michael E. McCullough of the University of Miami, have conducted research on gratitude. In one study, they asked all participants to write a few sentences each week, focusing on particular topics.

One group wrote about things they were grateful for that had occurred during the week. A second group wrote about things that had displeased them and the third wrote about events that had affected them (with no emphasis on them being positive or negative). After ten weeks, those who wrote about gratitude were more optimistic and felt better about their lives. Surprisingly, they also exercised more and had fewer visits to physicians than those who focused on sources of aggravation.

Another leading researcher in this field, Dr Martin E. P. Seligman, a psychologist at the University of Pennsylvania, tested the impact of various positive psychology interventions on 411 people, each compared with a control assignment of writing about early memories. When their week's assignment was to write and personally deliver a letter of gratitude to someone who had never been properly thanked for their kindness, participants immediately exhibited a huge increase in happiness scores. This impact was greater than that experienced from any other intervention, with benefits lasting for a month.

Write a journal!

Visualise how it would feel to starting every day in a positive mood, revitalised, ready to take on the world. Instead of psychologically replaying all your life's problems and hiding, you can choose to take control of your mind and focus on the good.

Having a clear mind is very important. Clearing your mind first thing in the morning and last thing before you go to bed at night can be one of the best habits you can develop. Criticising others and yourself and concentrating on problems come easily. For most of us, appreciation and focusing on the good take effort. By keeping a gratitude journal, you develop a practice that keeps you accountable for developing appreciation and enjoying happier days.

Writing your thoughts down every day helps you in many ways, from getting through mental obstacles and setting goals to remembering and thanking what you are grateful for. It gives you great insight and understanding of your life. Start your day by writing one thing you want to accomplish that day, one thing you are grateful for and one thing you may be struggling with. At the end of the day, revisit your journal and see if you accomplished your task, reflect on where your mind is and write down what went well and what you might want to do differently the next day to make it more productive. Once you have developed the habit of writing daily, you can expand on your entries by adding more to your lists.

How to keep a gratitude journal

Instead of thinking of random things to be grateful for each day, you could use the following categories as a guide:

1. Relations: an association that really helped you
2. A prospect that you have had today

3. Something great that happened or that you saw yesterday
4. Something simple near you (such as nice weather outside or a pen you are holding).

You could also focus on one category a day. Instead of trying to colour with every gratitude crayon in the box, just use a few. What if today you just focused on the relationships you are grateful for? You will find that having a day where you select a 'category' helps create gratitude ideas more quickly.

Ideas for your gratitude journal

Taking the categories one layer deeper, here are example prompts to get your mind going. Some of these will take some time to go past your initial resistance or self-criticism. Dig deeper. There are gems there!

Relationships:

1. What relationship am I grateful for?
2. What qualities do I appreciate in a co-worker?
3. What is the one quality I admire in my partner?
4. What positive quality have I picked up from my mother?
5. What positive quality have I picked up from my father?
6. What positive quality do I really admire about myself?
7. What positive qualities of a role model do I value?

Today's opportunities:

1. What is an opportunity I have today that most people don't that I can appreciate?

2. What one thing that is within my control that would make today great?
3. What is something I am better at today than I was yesterday?
4. What can I appreciate about today's weather?
5. What is one thing I appreciate about my health?
6. What do I appreciate about the career skills I have today?
7. What can I appreciate/accept about my financial situation?
8. What can I appreciate about my appearance today?

Past opportunities:

1. What is one good thing that occurred through the day?
2. What difficulty have I overcome that I appreciate about myself?
3. What did I appreciate about a former job?
4. What do I admire about my childhood?
5. What is a past experience that felt bad at the time that I can appreciate now?
6. What did I learn in school that I am grateful for?
7. What is one thing I appreciate about my ancestors that allows me to live the life I have?
8. What do I appreciate about the food I ate (or didn't eat) today?
9. What sight did I see yesterday that I found enjoyable?

General:

1. Here is one item I love. What do I love about it?
2. What do I appreciate about the house I live in?
3. What do I appreciate about the city I live in?

4. What do I appreciate about the country I live in?
5. What do I appreciate about the restaurants I frequent?
6. What is one piece of clothing I appreciate?
7. What do I appreciate about the music I listen to?
8. What is one thing I appreciate about my body?
9. What food do I really appreciate and why?

Several studies and research reveal that gratitude has many holistic benefits:

1. Showing gratitude opens the door to relationships. Appreciation goes a long way in winning friends and acquaintances. So, whether you thank a stranger for holding the door or you send a quick thank-you note to that co-worker who helped you with a project, acknowledging other people's contributions can lead to new opportunities. Writing down these small experiences helps create positive energy.
2. Grateful people experience fewer aches and pains and they report feeling healthier than other people, according to a 2012 study published in *Personality and Individual Differences*. Not surprisingly, grateful people are also more likely to take care of their health. They exercise more often and are more likely to attend regular check-ups with their doctors, which is likely to contribute further to longevity.
3. Gratitude reduces many toxic emotions, ranging from envy and resentment to frustration and regret. Robert A. Emmons, Ph.D., a leading gratitude researcher, has conducted multiple studies on the link between gratitude and well-being. His study and research assert that gratitude effectively increases happiness and reduces depression.

4. According to a 2012 study by the University of Kentucky, grateful people are more likely to behave in a positive and helpful and tend to promote social acceptance and friendship, even when others behave less kindly. Study participants who ranked higher on gratitude scales were less likely to retaliate against others even when given negative feedback.
5. According to a 2011 study published in *Applied Psychology: Health and Well-Being*, writing in a gratitude journal improved sleep. So, spending just 15 minutes jotting down a few grateful sentiments before bed may help you sleep better and longer.
6. A 2014 study published in the *Journal of Applied Sport Psychology* found that gratitude increased the athlete's self-esteem, which is essential to optimal performance.
7. Gratitude helps build mental strength. Research has shown gratitude not only reduces stress, but it may also play a major role in overcoming trauma. A 2006 study published in *Behavior Research and Therapy* found that Vietnam War veterans with higher levels of gratitude experienced lower rates of post-traumatic stress disorder. A 2003 study published in the *Journal of Personality and Social Psychology* found that gratitude was a major contributor to resilience following the terrorist attacks on September 11.

Gratitude prayer

Having a gratitude prayer that you can customise regularly by adding small things to show gratitude will not only uplift you but keep you in a positive frame of mind. You can make one on your own and say it every night before sleeping or even in times that you feel stressed and anxious. It doesn't have to be too long, just a small note also helps.

Here is a simple gratitude prayer by Kelli Mahoney:

'Thank you God, for the blessings you have bestowed on my life. You have provided me with more than I could ever have imagined. You have surrounded me with people who always look out for me. You have given me family and friends who bless me every day with kind words and actions. They lift me up in ways that keep my eyes focused on you and make my spirit soar.

'Also, thank you, God, for keeping me safe. You protect me from those things that seem to haunt others. You help me make better choices, and you have provided me with advisors that help me with the difficult decisions. You speak to me in so many ways so that I always know you are here.

'And God, I am so grateful for keeping those around me safe and loved. I hope that you provide me with the ability and sense to show them every day how much they matter. I hope that you give me the ability to give to them the same kindness they have provided to me. I am just so grateful for all of your blessings in my life, God. I pray that you remind me of just how lucky I am, and that you never allow me to forget to show my gratitude in prayer and returned kind acts. Thank you, God.'

3. Daily positive affirmations

Daily positive affirmations greatly improve our mindset. People use affirmations for diverse purposes, but affirmations are commonly used to encourage us to believe certain things about ourselves or about the world and our place within it. They are also used to help us create the truth we want in terms of making (or attracting) wealth, love, beauty, and happiness. Self-affirmations were first popularised in the 1920s and have since been proclaimed by coaches and self-help gurus around the world. But do they work?

According to Walter E. Jacobson, M.D., there is value in affirmations of this nature, because our subconscious mind plays a major role in the actualisation of our lives and the manifestation of our desires. What we believe about ourselves at a subconscious level, he says, can have a significant impact on the outcome of events.

At the most modest level, when we feel good about ourselves and have a positive attitude, our lives tend to run smoothly. Advocates of the 'law of attraction' often refer to this as raising our vibration such that when our vibration is positive, positive things—such as financial abundance, love and renewed health—are magnetically drawn to us.

On the other hand, when we feel bad about ourselves and have a negative attitude, we tend to get engrossed in self-defeating behaviours that may have negative outcomes, such as financial mishaps, interpersonal drama or acute or chronic illness.

And, on a much more practical level, recent scholarship from a team of researchers at Carnegie Mellon University suggests that self-affirmations actually buffer stress and improve problem-solving performance in underperforming and chronically stressed individuals.

What are affirmations?

Affirmations are easy-to-understand statements that are designed to create self-change in the individual using them. They inspire and even act as simple reminders. Affirmations bring our focus to our life goals throughout the day.

Here are some points to consider while writing effective affirmations.

1. Affirmations should be written in first person.

Begin your affirmations with the 'I'. These types of statements turn affirmations into statements of identity that are powerful promoters of self-change. Examples of 'I' statements would be, 'I am safe and confident speaking in public', 'I love eating healthy food', 'I love to exercise'.

2. Affirmations are written in a positive form.

Always state your affirmations in a positive way. For example, instead of saying, 'I no longer enjoy smoking cigarettes', you might say, 'I am completely free from cigarettes', or 'I am a healthy person and I love the way my body feels when I make healthy choices'.

3. Affirmations have an emotional element attached to them.

Instil your affirmations with feelings. Using expressive words in affirmations is important because of the association with our experiences. So instead of saying, 'I spend time with my aging parents', try saying, 'I feel such love and gratitude spending time with my mother and father'.

Affirmations are always written in the present tense.
Always write your affirmation like they are happening now. Write them as if they are already happening. This means affirming, 'I am happy and confident', instead of 'Two months from now, I will be happy and confident'.

This is where most people falter, because they feel silly writing or saying something that they actually don't yet believe—this is true at least at a conscious level. But remember, the purpose behind affirmations is to rewire your subconscious mind.

The most important thing in writing affirmations is not being caught in the how. Because if you believe that you are a certain way, you will—subconsciously—figure out a way to make it work.

You should also make a habit of regularly updating the affirmations. If you'd like to try your hand at writing your own, personal affirmations, there is an app called *Affirmable* that lets you easily create your own affirmations and work with them every day.

How do you use affirmations?

Once you've come up with a set of affirmations, you must use them. In order to be effective, affirmations must be used daily—at a minimum.

Some sources suggest that you think of your affirmations first thing in the morning and last thing at night. Others recommend putting your affirmations on note cards and leaving them in plain sight, such as on your bathroom mirror, the steering wheel on your car, your computer monitor or in your purse or wallet, so that you see them all the time.

Different people also have different modes of using affirmations. Others simply read or repeat affirmations from a list, a stack of cards or, most recently, from smartphone apps. Indeed, there are a number of phone apps for purchase that come pre-stocked with affirmations related to health, wealth and relationships.

4. Intermittent fasting: the 16:8 rule

Popularised by Martin Berkhan, Leangains or 16/8 is form of fasting where the fasting period is sixteen hours and the eating window is shortened to eight hours. During this time, you may eat as many meals as you like, with the most frequent iteration being three meals.

Designed specifically with training the mind and providing the means for that, the 16/8 method has specific post-workout suggestions and recommendations. In nearly all ways, it's the most sophisticated form of intermittent fasting.

This type of fasting stands out because it offers an advanced level of hormonal management. It supports weight loss and controls blood sugar and improves brain function and longevity. Eat a healthy diet during your eating period and drink calorie-free beverages such as water or unsweetened teas and coffee.

5. Water memory

According to scientists, a new perception of water can be formed. German scientists believe that as water travels, it picks up and stores information from all of the places that it has travelled through, which can thereby connect people to a lot of different places and sources of information depending on the water they drink.

The journey of water has even been compared to the human body. Each body is inimitable and has an individual DNA unlike any other. The human body is made up of 70 per cent water. Consequently, it can be assumed that human tears can hold a unique memory of an individual being. As the body's store of water holds a complete store of information linked to individual experience, it is possible that everyone is globally connected by the water in their bodies.

Water is known to have amazing healing powers. Putting in good intentions or very pure intentions into the water before you drink it can have a very powerful impact on your health and overall well-being. Every time we drink water, we have the ability to heal ourselves. Every time we eat and drink, we absorb life force from it, and this life force has an influence on how aligned we are spiritually and how balanced our life is.

A very useful exercise that you can perform to help yourself and our family stay hydrated while using water memory: add some lemon, cucumbers and mint leaves to a jar of water to flavour it and encourage every family member to drink water from this jar and say something nice for themselves every time they take a sip.

To conclude this chapter, it is very important to keep a balance in life by having a positive outlook, exercising your body and taking care of yourself.

SECTION THREE: RECIPES AND DIET PLANS

18

The Lifestyle Butter Coffee

---·---

WHEN IT COMES to butter coffee, I have to wonder where to start. Butter coffee is literally the reason I look forward to the mornings. It is also why I force myself to sleep: so that I can wake up and have my butter coffee! I have introduced many people to butter coffee, and each and every one of them is now hooked on it. I am going to tell you exactly how and why to make butter coffee. And I'll also reveal all the different variations of the beverage.

I know the name sounds super fancy. And it has also got multiple health benefits.

Hold on, one thing at a time. Let's begin with how to make it.

Basic butter coffee

Ingredients

Organic black coffee (Americano)
Cow ghee
Coconut oil

Process

Blend together 200 ml coffee, 1 tablespoon ghee and 1 tablespoon coconut oil for five seconds in a blender.

Collagen butter coffee

Ingredients

Organic black coffee
Cow ghee
Coconut oil
Collagen powder (type 1 and 3)

Process

Blend together 200ml black coffee, 1 tablespoon ghee, 1 tablespoon coconut oil and 1 scoop collagen powder for 5–10 seconds in a blender.

Advanced butter coffee

Ingredients

Organic black coffee
Cow ghee (A2)
Coconut oil
Collagen powder
Organic coconut milk or almond milk

Process

Blend all ingredients well together.

Anti-inflammatory butter coffee

This coffee is best for intermittent fasting. Whoever is on this diet can either break their fast with this coffee or have it when they get those terrible hunger pangs in the fasting window.

Ingredients

Organic black coffee
Cow ghee (A2)
Coconut oil
Collagen powder
Organic turmeric

Process

Blend together 250 ml black coffee, 1 tablespoon ghee, 1 tablespoon coconut oil, 1 scoop collagen and 1 teaspoon turmeric in a blender or mixer.

Now, these butter coffees are hands down the best thing you can have after your morning drink. You can also replace your breakfast with this coffee if you usually skip breakfast or if you don't like eating in the morning.

Here are its amazing benefits:

1. This fully stabilises your insulin levels for the day.
2. It prevent any spike in your blood sugar levels.
3. It puts your body into the fat-burning mode.
4. It works perfectly for your skin and hair.

5. It protects your gut lining.
6. This is a perfect treatment for PCOD, thyroid, diabetes or any hormonal disorder.
7. It helps in the absorption of your fat-soluble vitamins, i.e. A, D, E, K, and hence balances your hormones perfectly. I love to combine my advanced butter coffee with one peanut or almond butter truffle (homemade) as my pre-workout meal. This way I can be assured that my body burns the maximum fat during the workout.

So what are you waiting for? Start your day tomorrow with a butter coffee! Follow this routine for 30–45 days and see what it does to your body.

19

The Lifestyle Smoothies

SMOOTHIES ARE ONE of the best and my most favourite way to take in the daily dose of nutrients (mainly proteins and antioxidants). They are easy to make, carry, drink and nourish yourselves with. I love to replace my lunch with a super-filling and nourishing smoothie. It keeps me satiated, energetic and hydrated throughout the day. The main reason I love having a smoothie for lunch is that as a working woman, if I have a heavy lunch in the afternoons, I feel very drowsy and sleepy, which adversely affects my productivity, focus and concentration. On the other hand, a (big) glass of smoothie keeps me energetic and highly productive as it is easier on the digestive system as well.

In this chapter, we are going to talk about the basics of making a smoothie, so that you can whip up your smoothie blends and combinations at any time, using whichever ingredient is available in your kitchen. I will also share some of my favourite smoothie recipes towards the end of this chapter.

WHAT ARE THE BASIC INGREDIENTS OF A SMOOTHIE?

A smoothie should have one or more ingredients from each of the following categories:

1. Protein
Having a protein component in your smoothie keeps you energised for a longer period. At the same time, this is one of the best ways to get your daily dose of protein, which is very important in an Indian dietary lifestyle. You can go for a plant-based protein such as a good quality soy protein (provided you are not allergic to it), hemp protein, pea protein or brown rice protein. You can also go for sprouted-moong-based smoothies (sprouting lentils makes them easy for digestion and better for gut health).

2. Sweetener
I know most of you have sugar cravings around the afternoon time, especially when you are stressed at work and your blood sugar levels start dropping. This is the best time to curb these cravings with these super delicious smoothies containing the most nourishing and natural sugars. You can include any seasonal fruit of your choice (mango, dragon fruit, berries, papaya, pineapple, chikoo, banana and the list goes on) and dates (dates are a great source of iron, copper, manganese,

potassium and vitamin B6, and only two dates are enough to sweeten your smoothie). You can also try stevia leaves (if you want zero calorie intake from the sweetener as stevia has a zero glycaemic index).

3. Vegetables
Yes, I have always advised people to drink your veggies if you don't like eating them. Adding vegetables to smoothies make them rich in B-complex vitamins, antioxidants and chlorophyll, all of which are the best foods for the skin. You can include vegetable options such as spinach, kale, celery, coriander leaves, mint leaves, wheatgrass, carrots and the like.

4. Herbs and spices
These are my favourite additions to smoothies. They not only increase the nutrition value of the smoothie but also help in increasing your longevity. Include herbs and spices in your smoothie as they are known to reduce the oxidation (oxidative stress) in the body. You can use turmeric, cinnamon, cardamom, ginseng, ashwagandha, shatavari (all in powder form) and so on.

5. Nuts and seeds
Nuts and seeds further enhance the protein, mineral and omegas (omega 3,6,9) content of a smoothie. Here are the must-have nuts and seeds in your smoothies: almonds, walnuts, cashews, pecans, pumpkin seeds, flax seeds, sunflower seeds and chia seeds (white chia and black chia).

6. Milk base

Your smoothie becomes even more nutritious and lower in the glycaemic index if you add plant-based milk to it. You can go for almond milk, coconut milk or cashew milk. Nut milk is always the best option for people with diabetes, PCOD, irritable bowel syndrome (IBS/IBD) and lactose intolerance. So go for any one of these dairy-free options for your smoothie!

HOW DO YOU ADOPT SMOOTHIES AS A PART OF YOUR DAILY LIFESTYLE?

Smoothies need to be a part of your day-to-day lifestyle, just like your teas and coffees and snacks. Here's what you can do: find out that time of the day when your hunger pangs and cravings are at the peak and you end up eating the wrong food. This is exactly when you should be having your smoothie. You can also have it as a meal replacement (replace breakfast or lunch or dinner with any of your favourite smoothies).

Now let's take a look at some of my favourite smoothie recipes. Don't forget that you can make your own combinations now that you know the basic ingredients.

BASIC IMMUNITY-BOOSTING SMOOTHIE RECIPES:

Smoothie 1

Ingredients

    1 tablespoon strawberries

1 tablespoon blueberries
1 tablespoon raspberries
1 tablespoon mulberries
1 tablespoon chia seeds
2 small-sized bananas (elaichi banana)
1 tablespoon sunflower seeds
1 teaspoon cinnamon powder
100 ml almond or coconut milk

Process

Add all the ingredients to a blender and blend until you get a nice, thick paste. Then add some water according to the consistency that you want and blend well for 15–20 seconds.

Smoothie 2

Ingredients

½ avocado
1 bowl baby spinach
1 small-sized banana
350 ml almond milk
1 tablespoon pumpkin seeds
1 teaspoon haldi (turmeric)
1 scoop of any plant-based protein
1 teaspoon cinnamon powder

Process

Blend and add water according to the consistency that you want.

Smoothie 3

Ingredients

8–9 mixed dry fruits
½ apple
1 pineapple slice
1 teaspoon ashwagandha powder
350 ml coconut milk
1 teaspoon cinnamon powder
1 scoop of any plant-based protein

Process

Blend and add water according to the consistency that you want.

Smoothie 4

Ingredients

½ apple
½ avocado
a handful moong sprouts
a ½ inch ginger piece
cucumber
fresh tender coconut malai
½ teaspoon haldi

Process

Blend and add water according to the consistency that you want.

Smoothie 5

Ingredients

1 bowl blackberries, blueberries, cranberries, mulberries or strawberries
1 small banana
350 ml almond milk
1 tablespoon pumpkin seeds
1 teaspoon cinnamon powder
1 scoop of any plant-based protein

Process

Blend and add water according to the required consistency.

Smoothie 6

Ingredients

1 carrot
½ apple
8–9 mint leaves
7 almonds
1 teaspoon chia seeds
1 teaspoon haldi
250 ml coconut milk

Process

Blend and add water according to the required consistency.

Smoothie 7

Ingredients
- 1 mango
- 1 tablespoon chia seeds
- 1 cup almond milk
- 1 teaspoon cinnamon powder
- 1 tablespoon pumpkin seeds
- 1 tablespoon sunflower seeds
- ½ banana

Process

Blend and add water as per the required consistency.

Smoothie 8

Ingredients
- 1 tablespoon cooked oats
- 1 teaspoon cinnamon powder
- 2–3 dates
- 1 tablespoon pumpkin seeds
- 1 tablespoon sunflower seeds
- 1 cup almond milk
- 1 tablespoon raw chia seeds

Process

Blend well and add water according to the required consistency.

20

101 Diet Plans

I CANNOT EXPRESS how happy and excited I feel about sharing this chapter and these diet plans with you all. This chapter has 101 diet plans curated by me only for you to know that there's a lot that you can explore with eating healthy. You can follow a different diet plan every day and you still will have 100 more different ways of eating different foods. However, while following these diet plans, there are a few things that you need to know and remember. They are as follows:

1. I do not claim that these diet plans have any medicinal effect on the body.
2. If you have any existing health issues such as diabetes, hypertension, PCOD, thyroid, heart disease or any other

illness, kindly speak to your doctor before starting on any diet plan.
3. In each of these diet plans, I have mainly focused on the foods and ingredients themselves and have not mentioned the portions because I believe that you can decide what portions you want to consume. Also this way, you are free to explore these new ways of eating.
4. In the juices and smoothies, if you like any particular ingredient, you can always add more of it and if you don't like any ingredient, you can reduce its quantity. It's all about finding your own taste and health.
5. Kindly talk to your doctor before taking any health supplement suggested in this book or in the diet plans.
6. Some of the food items/meals may be repeated across plans, but every routine is unique in its own way.

Even a mid-morning drink or a mid-evening snack that you do differently can greatly impact your health, and the main purpose of this is to show you that there can be so many different ways of eating every day. So go ahead and enjoy your healthy lifestyle journey. I promise you won't have to look back ever again!

THE LIFESTYLE DIET PLAN NO. 1

(Detox diet plan)

Breakfast: 1 cup lemon/ginger/tulsi tea + 1 bowl quinoa upma or porridge

Mid-morning snack: 1 bowl pomegranate and carrots + 1 tbsp pumpkin and sunflower seeds + 5 almonds+ radish juice

Lunch: green smoothie (with any three different-coloured veggies)+ mixed dry fruits + 1 tsp coconut oil + dahi + some water

Mid-afternoon snack: plain celery or kale juice with black pepper and pink salt/rock salt

Dinner: boiled vegetable salad with moong dal or with tofu (any recipe of your choice)

THE LIFESTYLE DIET PLAN NO. 2

(Routine diet plan)

Upon waking up: 1 tsp turmeric + ½ tsp ACV in normal water

Breakfast: 1 cup black coffee (with 1 tsp ghee or coconut oil + 1 tsp haldi + 1 scoop collagen powder)

or

1 glass morning smoothie (1 banana + 1 tbsp overnight soaked oats + 5 soaked almonds + 1 tbsp mixed seeds + 1 tsp raw cacao powder + coconut malai or almond milk)

or

2 whole eggs bhurji

Mid-morning snack: 8 almonds + 5 walnuts + 1 cup green tea with lemon

Lunch: 1 ragi/jowar roti + 1 bowl dal + 1 bowl any seasonal cooked vegetable or grilled fish or egg curry/bhurji + 1 bowl raita

Mid-evening snack: 1 bowl roasted makhana chivda + 1 cup herbal tea

Dinner: 3–4 hours before sleeping; before 7:30 p.m.: 1 bowl sprouts usal + dal + 1 bowl dahi

THE LIFESTYLE DIET PLAN NO. 3

(Body-building diet with routine [time-wise schedule; you can modify according to your timings])

7:30 a.m.: wake up; 1 glass water (normal temp) with freshly squeezed lemon

7:45 a.m.: 1 banana + 1 bowl mixed dry fruits

8:00 a.m.: workout

Immediately after workout: 1 scoop plant-based protein powder in lukewarm water + 1 tsp coconut oil

9:45 a.m.: 1 cup (size of a coffee mug) warm water + 1 tsp cold-pressed coconut oil

10:00 a.m. (breakfast): 1 bowl moong dal chilla/daliya + 2–3 eggs omelette/boiled + 1 B-complex capsule

12:00 p.m.: black coffee with cinnamon powder + 1 fresh fruit (any)

12:50 p.m.: 1 cup warm water + 1 tsp cold-pressed coconut oil

1:00 p.m. (lunch): 1–2 bhakris + chicken curry/masala (your choice) + raita (homemade) + radish and onions

3:30 p.m.: black coffee/herbal tea with cinnamon powder +1 vitamin C tablet + 1 spirulina capsule

4:30 p.m.: green smoothie (banana + yoghurt + spinach + mixed seeds + dates + apple + any other vegetable)

5:00 p.m.: workout

Immediately after workout: 1 scoop protein powder with water (normal temp)

6:45 p.m.: 1 bowl of dahi + mixed dry fruits

8:00 p.m.: 1 cup warm water + 1 tsp cold-pressed coconut oil

8:10 p.m.: 1 bowl sprouted brown rice + 1 bowl fish curry + raw onions, tomatoes and radish

10:00 p.m.: some roasted peanuts, almonds and pistachios

11:00 p.m.: 1 cup green tea/herbal tea with freshly squeezed lemon

Before sleeping: 1 glass water with wheatgrass powder and lemon

Tip: Make sure you drink warm water or black tea during and around the meals.

THE LIFESTYLE DIET PLAN NO. 4

(Routine diet plan with timings)

6:15 a.m.: wake up; 1 glass wheatgrass powder in water (normal temperature) with lemon

6:30 a.m.: 1 banana

7:00 a.m.: workout

8:50 a.m.: 1 tsp cold-pressed coconut oil in warm water

9:00 a.m. (breakfast): 2–3 thalipith/paratha (with 1 tsp ghee) + pudina chutney + 1 small bowl dahi/2–3 boiled eggs (with yolk)

11:00 a.m.: 1 cup black tea or coffee + 1 apple/kiwi/pomegranate

1:45 p.m.: 1 tsp cold-pressed coconut oil in warm water

2:00 p.m. (lunch): bhakari + 1 bowl green leafy vegetable (any) + 1 bowl dal + raw tomato, onions and radish

4:00 p.m.: 1 cup green tea with cinnamon powder + 5 almonds + 5 walnuts + 2–3 dates

6:00 p.m.: 1 cup herbal tea + 5 cashew nuts

7:00 p.m.: 1 banana

7:30 p.m. to 8:30 p.m.: workout

9:00 p.m.: 1 tsp cold-pressed coconut oil in warm water

Before **dinner:** 1 probiotics capsule

9:10 p.m. (dinner): 1 bowl sprouted brown rice + 1 bowl any usual curry + raw radish

11:00 p.m.: 1 cup herbal tea/green tea

Before sleeping: 1 glass wheatgrass powder with lemon in water

THE LIFESTYLE DIET PLAN NO. 5

(Routine diet plan)

6:15 a.m.: wake up; 1 glass wheatgrass powder in water (normal temperature) with lemon

6:30 a.m.: 1 banana

7:00 a.m.: workout

8:50 a.m.: 1 tsp cold-pressed coconut oil in warm water

9:00 a.m. (breakfast): 1–2 dosas with coconut chutney

11:00 a.m.: 1 cup black tea/coffee + 1 apple/kiwi/pomegranate

1:45 p.m.: 1 tsp cold-pressed coconut oil in warm water

2:00 p.m. (lunch): 1–2 bowls sambar (cooked with lots of vegetables) + idli (quantity according to your hunger) + coconut chutney + raw tomato, onions and radish

4:00 p.m.: 1 cup green tea with cinnamon powder + 5 almonds + 5 walnuts + 2–3 dates

6:00 p.m.: 1 cup herbal tea + 5 cashew nuts

7:00 p.m.: 1 banana

7:30 p.m. to 8:30 p.m.: workout

9:00 p.m.: 1 tsp cold-pressed coconut oil in warm water

Before dinner: 1 probiotics capsule

9:10 p.m. (dinner): 1 bowl sprouted brown rice + 1 bowl plain dal/phodnanicha varan (dal tadka) + 1 tsp cow ghee + raw radish

11:00 p.m.: 1 cup herbal tea/green tea

Before sleeping: 1 glass wheatgrass powder with lemon in water

THE LIFESTYLE DIET PLAN NO. 6

(Routine diet plan)

6:15 a.m.: wake up; 1 glass wheatgrass powder in water (normal temperature) with lemon

6:30 a.m.: 1 banana

7:00 a.m.: workout

8:50 a.m.: 1 tsp cold-pressed coconut oil in warm water

9:00 a.m. (breakfast): 1–2 methi thalipith/paratha + 1 tsp cow ghee/2–3 boiled eggs (with yolk) cooked in ghee

Mid-morning snack: 1 seasonal fruit (any) + 1 cup herbal tea

1:45 p.m.: 1 tsp cold-pressed coconut in warm water

2:00 p.m. (lunch): 1 bhakri + 1 green leafy vegetable (any) + 1 bowl dal (any) + raw tomato, onions and radish

Mid-evening snack: 1 cup green tea/herbal tea with cinnamon powder + 5 almonds + 5 walnuts + 2 dates

7:00 p.m.: 1 tsp cold-pressed coconut oil in warm water + 1 probiotic capsule

7:30 p.m. (dinner): 1 bowl cauliflower soup + 250gm roasted fish with boiled vegetables + raw radish

11:00 p.m.: 1 cup herbal tea/green tea

Before sleeping: 1 glass wheatgrass powder with lemon in water

THE LIFESTYLE DIET PLAN NO. 7

(Diet for Indian fasts with timings)

6:15 a.m.: wake up; 1 glass wheatgrass powder in water (normal temperature) with lemon

8:50 a.m.: 1 tsp cold-pressed coconut oil in warm water

9:00 a.m. (breakfast): 1 bowl fresh seasonal fruits with chia seeds on top

11:00 a.m.: 1 cup black tea

1:45 p.m.: 1 tsp cold-pressed coconut in warm water

2:00 p.m. (lunch): 1 bowl shengdana curry + 1 bowl rajgira (amaranth leafy vegetable) curry + 1 bowl bhagar

4:00 p.m.: 1 cup green tea/herbal tea with cinnamon powder + 5 almonds + 5 walnuts + 2–3 dates + 1 rajgira (amaranth) ladoo

20 min before dinner: 1 tsp cold-pressed coconut oil in warm water

7:30 p.m. (dinner): 1 bowl shengdana curry + 1 bowl rajgira curry + 1 small bowl bhagar + sweet potatoes on the side

11:00 p.m.: 1 cup herbal tea/green tea

Before sleeping: 1 glass wheatgrass powder with lemon in water

THE LIFESTYLE DIET PLAN NO. 8

(Routine diet plan with timings

7:00 a.m.: wake up; 1 glass normal water + 1 tsp ACV

7:15 a.m.: 1 banana

7:00 a.m.: walking/any other exercise

9:30 a.m. (breakfast): 1 bowl oats/quinoa/daliya/parathas with 1 tsp ghee + 2 eggs (with yolk) boiled or half fried + 1 cup coffee/chai with stevia (no sugar or milk)

12:00 p.m.: 1 cup green tea/herbal tea + 1 fruit (any)

1:45 p.m. (lunch): 1 ragi roti + 1 bowl vegetable (any) + 1 bowl dal + raw radish, tomatoes and onions

4:15 p.m.: 1 cup green tea with lemon and cinnamon powder + 5 almonds + 5 walnuts + 5 cashew nuts + 5 pistachios

20 min before workout: 1 banana

4 hours before sleeping (dinner): 1 bowl brown rice + mushrooms/paneer/tofu/chicken curry + mixed vegetable salad (boiled)

Before sleeping: 1 glass of normal water + 1 tsp wheatgrass powder + 1 or ½ lemon

10:30/11:00 p.m.: sleep

THE LIFESTYLE DIET PLAN NO. 9

(Routine diet plan)

Upon waking up: 1 glass wheatgrass powder in water (normal temperature) with lemon

Workout

Post workout: 1 tsp cold-pressed coconut oil blended with black coffee

Breakfast: 2–3 ragi (nachni) idlis + coconut chutney + 1 tsp cow ghee + 2–3 boiled eggs (with yolk) + 1 B-complex capsule

Mid-morning snack: 1 cup black tea or coffee + 1 apple/kiwi/pomegranate

20 mins before lunch: 1tsp cold-pressed coconut oil in warm water

Lunch: 1 jowar roti + 1 bowl brinjal bharta + 1 bowl dal + raw tomato, onions and radish

Mid-evening snack: 1 cup green tea/herbal tea with cinnamon powder + 5 almonds + 5 walnuts + 2–3 dates

20 mins before dinner: 1 tsp cold-pressed coconut oil in warm water

Dinner: 1–2 bowl coconut-based chicken curry or any coconut-based soup with chicken broth + roasted chicken salad with boiled vegetables + raw radish on the sides

Post-dinner: 1 cup herbal tea/green tea

Before sleeping: 1 glass water with lemon

THE LIFESTYLE DIET PLAN NO. 10

(Routine diet plan with timings)

7:45 a.m.: wake up; 1 glass water (normal temperature) with ½ or 1 tsp ACV

8:30 a.m.: warm water with 1 tsp cold-pressed coconut oil

8:45 a.m. (breakfast): 1 bowl quinoa/oats with mixed seeds (chia seeds + flax seeds + pumpkin seeds + sunflower seeds) + 1 tsp cow ghee + 2 eggs with yolk (boiled)

11:30 a.m.: 1 cup green tea + 1 seasonal fruit

1:00 p.m.: warm water (1 cup) + 1 tsp cold-pressed coconut oil

1:15 p.m. (lunch): 1 nachni roti + 1 bowl bhindi + 1 bowl dal + raw radish and onions

5:00 p.m.: 1 cup herbal tea/green tea + 1 fruit (any) + 1 mixed dry fruits bowl (except dates and figs) + 1 spirulina

10 min before dinner: 1 tsp cold-pressed coconut oil with warm water

7:30 p.m. (dinner): 1 bowl sprouted brown rice + 1 bowl vegetable Thai curry (try having dinner as early as possible)

Before sleeping: 1 glass normal water with wheatgrass powder and lemon

THE LIFESTYLE DIET PLAN NO. 11

(Routine diet plan)

Upon waking up: 1 glass water (normal temperature) with ½ or 1 tsp ACV

20 min before breakfast: warm water with 1 tsp cold-pressed coconut oil

Breakfast: 1 bowl dal chilla with mixed seeds (chia seeds + flax seeds + pumpkin seeds + sunflower seeds) + 1 tsp cow ghee + 2 eggs with yolk (boiled)

Mid-morning snack: orange juice with sabza seeds

20 min before **lunch:** warm water (1 cup) + 1 tsp cold-pressed coconut oil

Lunch: 1 nachni roti + 1 green leafy vegetable/pumpkin curry + 1 bowl dal + raw onions

Mid-evening snack: 1 cup herbal tea/green tea + 1 mixed dry fruits bowl (except dates and figs

10 min before dinner: 1 tsp cold-pressed coconut oil with warm water

Dinner: 1 bowl tomato soup + 1 bowl boiled mixed lentils salad + sweet potatoes on the side (try having dinner as early as possible)

Before sleeping: 1 glass normal water with wheatgrass powder and lemon

THE LIFESTYLE DIET PLAN NO. 12

(Routine diet plan)

Morning: wake up; 1 glass water (normal temperature) + 1 tsp ACV

Before workout: 1 banana

Workout: 40 min walking/30 min running/weight training at the gym + some body weight exercises

10 min before breakfast: 1 tsp cold-pressed coconut oil in warm water

Breakfast: 1 bowl nachni porridge mixed seeds + 2 eggs (boiled/scrambled/omelette) + 1 cup black tea

Mid-morning snack: 1 cup green tea + 1 fruit (any) + 1 B-complex capsule + 1 tab celine

10 min before lunch: 1 tsp cold-pressed coconut oil in warm water

Lunch: 1 bowl brown rice chicken biryani or pulao + homemade raita (salted not sweet) + raw radish, tomato and onion

Mid-evening snack: 1 bowl mixed dry fruits (5 almonds + 5 walnuts + 5 cashews + 5 pistachios + 1–2 dates or figs) + 1 cup herbal tea (very important)

Evening workout: should mostly be body-weight-based or 40 min brisk walk

10 min before dinner: 1 tsp cold-pressed coconut oil in warm water

Dinner (between 6:30 and 7:30 p.m.): 1 bowl tomato soup + 1 bowl mixed sprouts salad with your favourite dressing + roasted sweet potatoes on the side

After-dinner drink (after about 1 hour): hibiscus/green tea + cinnamon powder and lemon

Before sleeping: 1 cup normal water with 1 tsp ACV

THE LIFESTYLE DIET PLAN NO. 13

(Routine diet plan)

Morning: wake up; 1 glass water (normal temperature) + 1 tsp ACV

Before workout: 1 banana

Workout: 40 min walking/30 min running/weight training at the gym + some body weight exercises

10 min before breakfast: 1 tsp cold-pressed coconut oil in warm water

Breakfast: 1 bowl daliya with mixed seeds/2 eggs (boiled/scrambled/omelette) + 1 cup black tea

Mid-morning snack: 1 cup tea (any) + 1 fruit (any) + 1 B complex capsule + 1 tab celine

10 min before lunch: 1 tsp cold-pressed coconut oil in warm water

Lunch: 1 nachni chapati/bhakri + 1 bowl of any green leafy vegetable + 1 bowl dal (any) + raw radish, tomato and onion on the side

Mid-evening snack: 1 bowl mixed dry fruits (5 almonds + 5 walnuts + 5 cashews + 5 pistachios + 1–2 dates or figs) + 1 cup herbal tea (very important)

Evening workout: should mostly be weight or body-weight-based or 40 min brisk walk

10 min before dinner: 1 tsp cold-pressed coconut oil in warm water

Dinner (between 6:30 and 7:30 p.m.): 1 bowl sprouted (soaked) brown rice + chicken Thai curry + roasted sweet potatoes on the side

After dinner drink (after about 1 hour): hibiscus/green tea + cinnamon powder and lemon

Before sleeping: 1 cup normal water with 1 tsp ACV

THE LIFESTYLE DIET PLAN NO. 14

(Routine diet plan)

Morning: wake up; 1 glass water (normal temperature) + 1 tsp ACV or ½ lemon

Before workout: 1 banana

Workout: 40 min walking/30 min running/weight training at the gym + some body weight exercises

10 min before breakfast: 1 tsp cold-pressed coconut oil in warm water

Breakfast: 1 bowl oats with mixed seeds +1 tsp cow ghee + 2 boiled eggs (with yolk)

Mid-morning snack: 1 cup green tea with cinnamon powder and lemon + 1 fruit (any)

10 mins before lunch: 1 tsp cold-pressed coconut oil in warm water

Lunch: 1 bhakri (nachni) + 1 bowl baingan bharta + 1 bowl dal + homemade garlic chutney + raw radish, tomato and onion

Mid-evening snack: 1 bowl mixed dry fruits (5 almonds + 5 walnuts+ 5 cashews + 5 pistachios + 1–2 dates or figs) + 1 cup herbal tea (very important)

Before evening workout: 1 banana

Evening workout: should mostly be body-weight-based

In case of no workout, have 1 glass buttermilk with rock salt/pink salt

10 min before dinner: 1 tsp cold-pressed coconut oil in warm water

Dinner: 1 bowl tomato soup or shorba + moong dal usal/steamed fish + homemade pickles or chutney on the side + raw radish, tomato and onion

Before sleeping: 1 cup green tea with cinnamon powder and lemon

THE LIFESTYLE DIET PLAN NO. 15

(Routine diet plan)

Morning: wake up; 1 glass water (normal temperature) + 1 tsp ACV or ½ lemon

Before workout: 1 banana

Workout: 40 min walking/30 min running/weight training at the gym + some body weight exercises

10 min before breakfast: 1 tsp cold-pressed coconut oil in warm water

Breakfast: 1–2 palak thalipith/paratha + pudina chutney + 1 tsp cow ghee with or without 2 boiled eggs (with yolk)

Mid-morning snack: 1 cup green tea with cinnamon powder and lemon + 1 fruit (any)

10 min before lunch: 1 tsp cold-pressed coconut oil in warm water

Lunch: 1 khapali gehu chapati + 1 bowl of any green leafy vegetable + 1 bowl dal + raw radish, tomato and onion

Mid-evening snack: 1 bowl mixed dry fruits (5 almonds + 5 walnuts+ 5 cashews + 5 pistachios + 1–2 dates or figs) + 1 cup herbal tea (very important)

Before evening workout: 1 banana

Evening workout: should mostly be weight or body-weight-based

In case of no workout, have 1 glass buttermilk with rock salt/pink salt

10 min before dinner: 1 tsp cold-pressed coconut oil in warm water

Dinner: 1 bowl mushroom soup + boiled chicken or tofu salad (use boiled vegetables along with your favourite seasoning) + homemade pickles or chutney on the side + raw radish, tomato and onion

Before sleeping: 1 cup green tea with cinnamon powder and lemon

THE LIFESTYLE DIET PLAN NO. 16

(Routine fat loss diet plan)

Upon waking up: 1 tsp ACV in normal water

20 min before breakfast: Cold-pressed coconut oil in warm water

Breakfast: 2 whole eggs + 1 nachni or mixed dal thalipith

Mid-morning snack: 1 glass green smoothie

20 min before lunch: 1 tsp organic cold-pressed coconut oil in green tea

Lunch: 1 bowl chicken curry + 1 bowl of any green leafy vegetable + steamed broccoli + raw onion, tomato and radish

Mid-evening snack: 1 coconut water + malai + 1 bowl roasted mixed seeds

20 min before dinner: 1 tsp cold-pressed coconut oil in warm water

Dinner (3 hours before sleeping): 150 gm grilled fish or mixed sprouts + 1 bowl stir fried broccoli, bell peppers, carrots, onions and garlic

Post dinner drink: 1 cup herbal tea with lemon

Sleep

Important health tip: Develop a habit of eating saunf (fennel seeds) after every meal. This will significantly balance your digestive process and also help in weight loss.

THE LIFESTYLE DIET PLAN NO. 17

(Routine diet plan with timings)

7:30 a.m.: wake up; 1 tsp raw ACV + 1 tsp haldi in normal water

8:00 a.m.: 8 almonds + 8 walnuts soaked in water

Pre-workout snack: 1 banana + 1 cup black coffee

9:00 a.m.: workout (cardio)

10:30 a.m.: 3 whole eggs + 2 eggs bhurji (with yolk) + thalipith (nachni + brown rice + cabbage) + 1 tsp ghee on it

12:00 p.m.: 1 glass green juice: celery + asparagus + kale + black pepper + rock salt + lemon

1:40 p.m.: 1 cup green tea with 1 tsp organic cold-pressed coconut oil

2:00 p.m. (lunch): 1 bowl carrot and pumpkin soup + 250 gm steamed fish with mixed vegetables + raw onion, tomato and radish

4:00 p.m.: roasted mixed seeds (flax + sunflower + pumpkin + chia+ hemp + watermelon; roasted with black pepper)

6:00 p.m.: 1 glass wheatgrass juice with 3 tsp chia seeds (sabza seeds) + 1 spirulina tablet

7:30 p.m.: 1 cup black coffee with 1 tsp coconut oil + 5 cashews + 5 pistachios + 5 walnuts + 5 hazelnuts (soaked in water)

8:00 p.m.: weight training

9:00 p.m. (dinner): 1 bowl mushroom soup (shitake mushrooms preferably) + 1 bowl mixed sprouts usal + 1 bowl cooked broccoli, bell peppers, tomatoes

10:30 p.m.: 1 cup green tea or herbal tea with cinnamon powder and lemon

12:30 p.m.: sleep

Important health tip: Develop a habit of eating saunf (fennel seeds) after every meal. This will significantly balance your digestive process and also help in weight loss.

THE LIFESTYLE DIET PLAN NO. 18
(Detox diet plan)

Breakfast: lemon/ginger/tulsi tea + 1 bowl quinoa upma

Mid-morning snack: juice made with pomegranate + carrots + pumpkin + chia seeds + radish

Lunch: green smoothie (spinach + cucumber + banana + almonds + mixed seeds + 1 tsp coconut oil + homemade yoghurt + water)

Mid-afternoon snack: 1 bowl mixed nuts (almonds + walnuts + apricots + cashews and pistachios + 1 glass cucumber + kale + celery + chia seeds juice

Dinner (between 7:00 and 7:30 p.m.): boiled vegetable salad with moong dal or with tofu or mushrooms

Post dinner drink: ginger and cinnamon tea with some lemon

Before sleeping: 1 glass plain water with 1 tsp ACV

THE LIFESTYLE DIET PLAN NO. 19

(Routine diet plan)

Morning: wake up; 1 glass water (normal temperature) + 1 tsp raw unfiltered ACV

10 min before breakfast: 1 tsp cold-pressed coconut oil in warm water

Breakfast: 2 eggs omelette + nachni/ragi roti + 1 tsp ghee

Mid-morning snack: 1 cup green tea with cinnamon powder and lemon + 1 fruit (any)

10 min before lunch: 1 tsp cold-pressed coconut oil in warm water

Lunch: 1 bowl sprouted/soaked brown rice + 1 bowl fish curry (coconut-based) + raw radish, onion and tomato on the side

Mid-evening snack: 1 bowl mixed dry fruits (5 almonds + 5 walnuts + 5 cashews + 5 pistachios + 1–2 dates or figs) + 1 cup herbal tea (very important)

Before evening workout: 1 banana

Evening workout: should mostly be weight or body-weight-based

10 min before dinner: 1 tsp cold-pressed coconut oil in warm water

Dinner (between 7:00 and 7:30 p.m.): 1 bowl moong sprouts salad + 1 bowl cooked bhindi + homemade pickles or chutney on the side + raw radish, tomato and onion

Before sleeping: 1 cup green tea with cinnamon powder and lemon

THE LIFESTYLE DIET PLAN NO. 20

(Detox diet plan)

Upon waking up: 1 glass water with 1 tsp ACV

Breakfast: lemon/ginger/tulsi tea + 1 bowl oats (no milk) + 5 walnuts

Mid-morning snack: smoothie with spinach + banana + mixed seeds + walnuts + yoghurt (homemade) + water

Lunch: vegetables salad with mushrooms and paneer or tofu + homemade buttermilk (2 glasses)

Mid-afternoon snack: juice made with celery/kale/cucumber + black pepper + flax seeds + rock/pink salt

Dinner (between 7:00 and 7:30 p.m.): boiled vegetable soup + sprouts (any; roasted or normally cooked) with pickles (homemade)

Post dinner drink: ginger + cinnamon tea with some lemon

Before sleeping: 1 glass water with ACV

THE LIFESTYLE DIET PLAN NO. 21

(Routine diet plan)

Breakfast: lemon/ginger/tulsi/herbal tea + 1 bowl daliya

Mid-morning snack: green juice made with green leafy veggies + flax and pumpkin seeds + black pepper + rock salt (if needed)

Lunch: 1 bowl sprouted or soaked brown rice + 1 bowl dal (yellow or black) + 1 tsp ghee (homemade preferably)

Mid-afternoon snack: juice made with carrots + radish + chia seeds + flax seeds + 1–2 dates

Dinner (between 7:00 and 7:30 p.m.): mixed sprouts soup + sautéed broccoli and bell peppers + homemade chutney on the side

Post-dinner drink: ginger + cinnamon tea with lemon

Before sleeping: 1 glass water with 1 tsp ACV

Tips:

1. Have three litres of water in a day.
2. Stick to your routine and do not skip meals or mess up the combinations.
3. If you want you can reduce the portion sizes, but do not entirely skip any meal or food item.
4. Be happy and peaceful and enjoy the process of eating healthy!
5. Take a walk 20 min after every meal. This will keep your body activity at a good level.

6. Dinner should *always* be 4–5 hours before sleeping.
7. Meditate and practice gratitude journaling daily!
8. Do not count your calories or starve yourself. Eat meal portions according to your hunger and your state of mind.

THE LIFESTYLE DIET PLAN NO. 22

(Routine diet plan)

Upon waking up: 1 glass ACV in normal water

Before breakfast: 1 tsp cold-pressed coconut oil in warm water

Breakfast: 1 bowl quinoa with mixed seeds + 1 egg with yolk (either boiled or omelette) + 1 tsp cow ghee

Mid-morning snack: 1 cup green tea + 1 fruit (any)

10 min before lunch: 1 tsp cold-pressed coconut oil in warm water

Lunch: 1–2 ragi rotis + 1 bowl dal

3:30 p.m.: 1 cup green tea/herbal tea + 2–3 dates + 5 almonds + 5 walnuts + 5 cashew nuts

5:45 p.m.: makhana chivda/omelette

15 min before dinner: 1 tsp cold-pressed coconut oil in warm herbal tea

Before 7:30 p.m. (dinner): 1 bowl sprouted brown rice + mushroom curry (tomato-based) + raw radish, tomato and onion

Before sleeping: 1 glass wheatgrass powder in normal water and lemon

THE LIFESTYLE DIET PLAN NO. 23

(Routine diet plan)

Morning: wake up; 1 glass water (normal temperature) + 1 tsp ACV

Before workout: 1 banana

Workout: 40 min walking/30 min running/weight training at the gym + some body weight exercises

10 min before breakfast: 1 tsp cold-pressed coconut oil in warm water

Breakfast: 2 wholegrain sourdough bread slices toasted in ghee + cheese + 2 eggs with yolk (omelette/boiled/scrambled)

Mid-morning snack: 1 cup fennel digestive tea + 1 fruit (any)

10 min before lunch: 1 tsp cold-pressed coconut oil in warm water

Lunch: 1 bowl sprouted (soaked) brown rice + 1 bowl chicken curry (any) + raw radish, tomato and onion on the side

Mid-evening snack: 1 bowl mixed dry fruits (5 almonds + 5 walnuts + 5 cashews + 5 pistachios + 1–2 dates or figs) + 1 cup herbal tea (very important)

Evening workout: should mostly be weight or body-weight-based or 40 min brisk walk

10 min before dinner: 1 tsp cold-pressed coconut oil in warm water

Dinner (between 6:30 and 7:30 p.m.): 1 bowl mushroom or cauliflower soup + grilled fish salad (boiled veggies with the salad with your favourite dressing) + raw radish, tomato and onion on the side

After-dinner drink (after about 1 hour): hibiscus/green tea + cinnamon powder and lemon

Before sleeping: 1 cup normal water with 1 tsp ACV

THE LIFESTYLE DIET PLAN NO. 24

(Routine diet plan)

Morning: wake up; 1 glass water (normal temperature) + 1 tsp ACV

Before workout: 1 banana

Workout: 40 min walking/30 min running/weight training at the gym + some body weight exercises

10 min before breakfast: 1 tsp cold-pressed coconut oil in warm water

Breakfast: 1 bowl quinoa upma with mixed seeds + 2 eggs (boiled/scrambled/omelette) + 1 cup black tea

Mid-morning snack: 1 cup tea (any) + 1 fruit (any)

10 min before lunch: 1 tsp cold-pressed coconut oil in warm water

Lunch: 1 nachni bhakri/roti + 1 bowl of any green leafy vegetable + 1 bowl dal + raw radish, tomato and onion on the side

Mid-evening snack: 1 bowl mixed dry fruits (5 almonds + 5 walnuts+ 5 cashews + 5 pistachios + 1–2 dates or figs) + 1 cup herbal tea (very important)

Evening workout: should mostly be weight or body-weight-based or 40 min brisk walk

10 min before dinner: 1 tsp cold-pressed coconut oil in warm water

Dinner (between 6:30 and 7:30 p.m.): 1 bowl tomato soup + egg whites salad (add boiled veggies to the salad with your favourite dressing) + raw radish, tomato and onion on the side

After dinner drink (after about 1 hour): hibiscus/green tea + cinnamon powder and lemon

Before sleeping: 1 cup normal water with 1 tsp ACV

THE LIFESTYLE DIET PLAN NO. 25

(Routine diet plan)

Morning: wake up; 1 glass water (normal temperature) + 1 tsp ACV + ½ tsp haldi

Before workout: 1 banana

Workout: 40 min walking/30 min running/weight training at the gym + some body weight exercises

10 min before breakfast: 1 tsp cold-pressed coconut oil in warm water

Breakfast: 1 bowl oats with banana and dark chocolate + 2 eggs with yolk (boiled) + 1 cup black tea

Mid-morning snack: 1 cup green tea (any) + 1 fruit (any)

10 min before lunch: 1 tsp cold-pressed coconut oil in warm water

Lunch: 1 bowl sprouted (soaked) brown rice + 1 bowl rajma or chavali curry + raw radish, tomato and onion on the side

Mid-evening snack: 1 bowl mixed dry fruits (5 almonds + 5 walnuts+ 5 cashews + 5 pistachios + 1–2 dates or figs) + 1 cup herbal tea (very important)

Evening workout: should mostly be weight or body-weight-based or 40 min brisk walk

10 min before dinner: 1 tsp cold-pressed coconut oil in warm water

Dinner (between 6:30 and 7:30 p.m.): 1 bowl mushroom soup + 1 bowl grilled or sautéed tofu salad with lots of veggies

After-dinner drink (after about 1 hour): hibiscus/green tea + cinnamon powder and lemon

Before sleeping: 1 cup normal water with 1 tsp ACV

THE LIFESTYLE DIET PLAN: 26

(Routine diet plan)

Morning: wake up; 1 glass water (normal temperature) + 1 tsp ACV

Before workout: 1 apple or orange

Workout: 40 min walking/30 min running/weight training at the gym + some body weight exercises

10 min before breakfast: 1 tsp cold-pressed coconut oil in warm water

Breakfast: 2 eggs with yolk (omelette/boiled/scrambled) + 1 cup black tea

Mid-morning snack: 1 cup tea (any) + 1 fruit (any)

10 min before lunch: 1 tsp cold-pressed coconut oil in warm water

Lunch: 1 nachni roti/bhakri + 1 bowl of any green leafy vegetable + 1 bowl any usal or dal + raw radish, tomato and onion on the side + homemade chutney or pickle (optional)

Mid-evening snack: 1 bowl mixed dry fruits (5 almonds + 5 walnuts+ 5 cashews + 5 pistachios + 1–2 dates or figs) + 1 cup herbal tea (very important)

Evening workout: should mostly be weight or body-weight-based or 40 min brisk walk

10 min before dinner: 1 tsp cold-pressed coconut oil in warm water

Dinner (between 6:30 and 7:30 p.m.): 1 bowl chicken salad with boiled veggies and tahini dressing + roasted sweet potatoes on the side

After-dinner drink (after about 1 hour): hibiscus/green tea + cinnamon powder and lemon

Before sleeping: 1 cup normal water with 1 tsp ACV

THE LIFESTYLE DIET PLAN NO. 27

(Routine diet plan)

Morning: wake up; 1 glass water (normal temperature) + 1 tsp ACV

Before workout: 1 banana

Workout: 40 min walking/30 min running/weight training at the gym + some body weight exercises

10 min before breakfast: 1 tsp cold-pressed coconut oil in warm water

Breakfast: 1–2 whole wheat sourdough bread toasted in ghee with some cheese + 2 eggs (boiled/scrambled/omelette) + 1 cup black tea

Mid-morning snack: 1 cup tea (any) +1 fruit (any)

10 min before lunch: 1 tsp cold-pressed coconut oil in warm water

Lunch: 1 nachni bhakri/chapati + 1 bowl of any green leafy vegetable + 1 bowl dal + raw radish, tomato and onion on the side

Mid-evening snack: 1 bowl mixed dry fruits (5 almonds + 5 walnuts+ 5 cashews + 5 pistachios + 1–2 dates or figs) + 1 cup herbal tea (very important)

Evening workout: should mostly be weight or body-weight-based or 40 min brisk walk

10 min before dinner: 1 tsp cold-pressed coconut oil in warm water

Dinner (between 6:30 and 7:30 p.m.): 1 bowl mushroom or cauliflower soup + sprouted moong salad (boiled veggies for the salad with your favourite dressing) + raw radish, tomato and onion on the side

After-dinner drink (after about 1 hour): hibiscus/green tea + cinnamon powder and lemon

Before sleeping: 1 cup normal water with 1 tsp ACV

THE LIFESTYLE DIET PLAN NO. 28

(Routine diet plan)

Morning: wake up; 1 glass water (normal temperature) + 1 tsp ACV

Before workout: 1 banana

Workout: 40 min walking/30 min running/weight training at the gym + some body weight exercises

10 min before breakfast: 1 tsp cold-pressed coconut oil in warm water

Breakfast: 1–2 dosas with coconut chutney + 2 eggs (boiled/scrambled/omelette) + 1 cup black tea

Mid-morning snack: 1 cup tea (any) + 1 fruit (any)

10 min before lunch: 1 tsp cold-pressed coconut oil in warm water

Lunch: 3–4 idlis + coconut chutney + 1–2 bowls sambar (cooked with mixed dals and lots of veggies) + raw radish, tomato and onion on the side

Mid-evening snack: 1 bowl mixed dry fruits (5 almonds + 5 walnuts + 5 cashews + 5 pistachios + 1–2 dates or figs) + 1 cup herbal tea (very important)

Evening workout: should mostly be weight or body-weight-based or 40 min brisk walk

10 min before dinner: 1 tsp cold-pressed coconut oil in warm water

Dinner (between 6:30 and 7:30 p.m.): 1 bowl grilled chicken salad with only green veggies (sautéed or boiled) with your favourite dressing + roasted sweet potatoes on the side

After-dinner drink (after about 1 hour): hibiscus/green tea + cinnamon powder and lemon

Before sleeping: 1 cup normal water with 1 tsp ACV

THE LIFESTYLE DIET PLAN NO. 29

(Routine diet plan)

Morning: wake up; 1 glass water (normal temperature) + 1 tsp ACV

Before workout: 1 banana

Workout: 40 min walking/30 min running/weight training at the gym + some body weight exercises

10 min before breakfast: 1 tsp cold-pressed coconut oil in warm water

Breakfast: 1 bowl nachni porridge + mixed seeds + 2 eggs (boiled/scrambled/omelette) + 1 cup black tea

Mid-morning snack: 1 cup green tea + 1 fruit (any)

10 min before lunch: 1 tsp cold-pressed coconut oil in warm water

Lunch: 1 bowl brown rice chicken biryani or pulao + homemade raita (salted not sweet) + raw radish, tomato and onion on the side

Mid-evening snack: 1 bowl mixed dry fruits (5 almonds + 5 walnuts+ 5 cashews + 5 pistachios + 1–2 dates or figs) + 1 cup herbal tea (very important)

Evening workout: should mostly be weight or body-weight-based or 40 min brisk walk

10 min before dinner: 1 tsp cold-pressed coconut oil in warm water

Dinner (between 6:30 and 7:30 p.m.): 1 bowl tomato soup + 1 bowl mixed sprouts salad with your favourite dressing + roasted sweet potatoes on the side

After-dinner drink (after about 1 hour): hibiscus/green tea + cinnamon powder and lemon

Before sleeping: 1 cup normal water with 1 tsp ACV

Tips:

1. Have three litres of water in a day.
2. Stick to your routine and do not skip meals or mess up the combinations.
3. If you want you can reduce the portion sizes, but do not entirely skip any meal or food item.
4. Be happy and peaceful and enjoy the process of eating healthy!
5. Take a walk 20 min after every meal. This will keep your body activity at a good level.
6. Dinner should *always* be 4–5 hours before sleeping.
7. Meditate and practice gratitude journaling daily!
8. Do not count your calories or starve yourself. Eat meal portions according to your hunger and your state of mind.

THE LIFESTYLE DIET PLAN NO. 30

(Routine diet for fat loss)

Upon waking up: 1 glass water or fresh wheatgrass juice with 1 tsp turmeric and 1 tbsp raw unfiltered ACV

Before morning exercise: 1 cup butter coffee

Workout followed by meditation

Breakfast: smoothie + 1 dosa or 2 idlis with coconut chutney

Mid-morning snack: 1 cup herbal tea with lemon + 1 bowl roasted makhana

Lunch: 1 bowl mixed veggies (cooked in dal like sambar) or 1 bowl veggies and 1 bowl dal + raw tomato, onion and radish on the side

Mid-evening snack: 1 cup herbal tea with lemon + 1 bowl soaked mixed seeds

Evening or post-dinner walk and meditation

Dinner: 1 bowl soup (any of your choice) + 1 bowl cooked sprouts + raw salad on the side

Before sleeping: 1 glass water with 1 tsp raw unfiltered ACV

Important health tip: Develop a habit of eating saunf (fennel seeds) after every meal. This will significantly balance your digestive process and also help in weight loss.

THE LIFESTYLE DIET PLAN NO. 31

(Routine diet plan)

Morning: wake up; 1 glass wheatgrass juice with ½ tsp raw unfiltered ACV and 1 tsp organic haldi

Before morning walk or Surya Namaskar: 5 almonds + 3 walnut halves soaked in water

1 hour walk or Surya Namaskar followed by 15 min meditation

Breakfast: 1 bowl urad dal and brown rice dosa (fermented overnight) + 1 cup lemon + basil + lemongrass tea

Mid-morning snack: 1 slice of papaya with 1 glass lemon water ½ lemon and plain water without sugar)

Lunch: millet (any) upma with lots of vegetables + 1 glass buttermilk

Mid-evening snack: 1 cup mixed seeds (flax seeds, chia seeds, pumpkin seeds and sunflower seeds) + 1 cup herbal tea

Evening walk for 1 hour

Dinner: 1 bowl cauliflower soup + 1 bowl carrots, sprouted moong and bean salad (cooked)

Before sleeping: 1 glass water with ½ tsp ACV

Important health tip: Develop a habit of eating saunf (fennel seeds) after every meal. This will significantly balance your digestive process and also help in weight loss.

THE LIFESTYLE DIET PLAN NO. 32

(Routine diet plan)

Morning: wake up; 1 glass water with 1 tsp raw unfiltered ACV + 1 tsp organic haldi

Before morning walk or Surya Namaskar: 5 almonds soaked in water

1 hour walk or Surya Namaskar followed by 15 min meditation

10–15 min before breakfast: 1 cup black coffee with coconut oil (½ tbsp)

Breakfast: moong thalipith or 1 dosa (or 2 idlis) + homemade coconut chutney on the side

Mid-morning snack: 1 cup green tea or herbal tea + 1 whole fruit (any seasonal)

Lunch: 1 bowl red rice/1 bhakri + 1 bowl mixed vegetable curry + raw tomato, cucumber, carrot and onion on the side

Mid-evening snack: 1 glass orange juice with sabza seeds

Evening walk for 1 hour

Dinner: 1 bowl cooked or sautéed vegetables + 1 bowl sprouts and raw salad on the side

Sleep

Important health tip: Develop a habit of eating saunf (fennel seeds) after every meal. This will significantly balance your digestive process and also help in weight loss.

THE LIFESTYLE DIET PLAN NO. 33

(Routine diet plan)

Upon waking up: 1 glass plain water with 1 tsp ACV

Before workout: 6–7 soaked almonds

1 hour walk

15–20 min meditation

Before breakfast: 1 tsp cold-pressed coconut oil in warm water

Breakfast: 1–2 dosas/uttapam + coconut chutney + 1 tsp cow ghee + 1 boiled egg (with yolk)

Mid-morning snack: herbal tea + 1 fruit (any)

Lunch: 1 bowl brown rice (soaked in water for at least 4 hours) + 1 bowl cooked vegetables + 1 bowl dal (yellow or black) + raw radish, tomato and onion

Post lunch: 1 glass homemade buttermilk with rock salt

Mid-evening snack: mixed dry fruits bowl (5 almonds + 5 walnuts + 5 cashews + 5 pistachios)

Evening walk for 1 hour

Dinner: 1 bowl quinoa pulao with vegetables (you can add any Indian masala if you like) + homemade pickle/chutney on the side + raw radish, tomato and onion

Before sleeping: 1 cup green tea with cinnamon powder and some lemon juice

THE LIFESTYLE DIET PLAN NO. 34

(Smoothie detox [for Indian fasts])

Upon waking up: 1 glass normal water with 1 tbsp ACV

Breakfast: 1 glass morning smoothie made with berries + banana+ almond milk + pumpkin seeds + 1 tsp cinnamon powder

Mid-morning snack: 1 cup almond tea + 1 bowl mixed seeds and nuts

Lunch: smoothie (mixed dry fruits+ apple+ papaya +½ tsp spirulina (optional) + 7–8 almonds + 1 cup homemade dahi + 1 tsp cinnamon powder)

Mid-evening snack: detox juice made with (pomegranate + chia seeds + sunflower seeds + flax seeds + pumpkin seeds + black or Himalayan salt + lemon)

or

Roasted makhanas with 1 cup almond tea

Dinner (3–4 hours before sleeping): Smoothie (papaya + strawberries + pistachios + 7–8 almonds + pumpkin seeds + fresh coconut malai + 1 tbsp dahi)

Before sleeping: 1 tbsp ACV in normal water

Snacking options:

1. 1 bowl roasted makhanas with rock salt or black salt
2. Sweet potatoes roasted in 1 tsp ghee and turmeric
3. All dry fruits and nuts

THE LIFESTYLE DIET PLAN NO. 35

(Diet plan for Indian fasts)

Breakfast: 1 cup butter coffee with 10 soaked almonds

Lunch: 1 bowl roasted makhana with 1 bowl freshly cut fruits (any seasonal)

Mid-evening snack: 1 glass orange juice with 1 tbsp sabza seeds

Dinner: 1 bowl sweet potatoes roasted in ghee and 1 tsp turmeric + rock salt + 8 walnut halves

THE LIFESTYLE DIET PLAN NO. 36

(Routine diet plan)

Upon waking up: 1 glass water (normal temp) with 1 tsp ACV

Breakfast: lemon/ginger/tulsi tea + 1–2 moong dal chilla or dosas + 5 almonds+ 5 walnuts

Mid-morning snack: 1 glass orange juice with sabza seeds

Lunch: 1 nachni dosa or bhakri + 1 bowl of any green leafy vegetable + 1 bowl dal + radish koshimbir (raita) on the side

Mid-evening snack: 1 cup black coffee with 1 tsp coconut oil + 1 small bowl mixed seeds

Dinner: 1 bowl asparagus/tomato/broccoli/spinach soup + 1 bowl cooked sprouts/grilled fish with lots of vegetables

Before sleeping: 1 glass water with 1 tsp ACV

THE LIFESTYLE DIET PLAN NO. 37

(Routine diet plan)

Upon waking up: 1 glass water with 1 tsp ACV + 1 tsp turmeric

Before workout or walk: 5 almonds + 5 walnuts (soaked)

Morning walk or workout for 60 min

Breakfast: 2 whole eggs bhurji or omelette cooked in ghee or 1–2 dosas (50% brown rice + 50% urad dal) with coconut chutney + 1 cup green tea with lemon and a pinch of cinnamon powder

Mid-morning snack: 1 glass celery juice with lemon and black pepper

Lunch: 1 ragi bhakri or dosa + 1 bowl of any green leafy vegetable + 1 bowl chicken or fish curry + raw onion, tomato, radish and cucumber on the side

Mid-evening snack: 1 bowl of mixed seeds + 1 cup coconut oil coffee

Dinner (4 hours before sleeping): 1 bowl sautéed veggies + 1 bowl cooked sprouts or dal or mushrooms on the side

Post-dinner walk: 40 min

Before sleeping: 1 glass water (normal temp) with 1 tsp ACV

THE LIFESTYLE DIET PLAN NO. 38

(Intermittent fasting)

11:00 a.m.: 1 glass normal water + 1 tbsp ACV

Breakfast: 1 glass morning smoothie (green apple + banana + almond milk + pumpkin seeds + 1 tsp cinnamon powder)

Lunch: 1 bowl cooked sprouts with 1 bowl vegetables (cooked)

Mid-evening snack: 1 cup butter coffee with 1 bowl mixed seeds

Dinner (6:30 p.m.): smoothie with carrots + cucumber + banana + coconut malai + water

Before sleeping: 1 tsp ACV in normal water

THE LIFESTYLE DIET PLAN NO. 39

(Detox diet)

Upon waking up: 1 glass water (normal temp) + 1 tsp raw unfiltered ACV

Breakfast: lemon/ginger/tulsi tea + 1–2 moong dal chilla + 5 almonds + 5 walnuts

Mid-morning snack: 1 glass orange juice with sabza seeds

Lunch: vegetable salad with mushrooms + homemade buttermilk (2 glasses)

Mid-afternoon snack: dahi (homemade) + 1 bowl mixed seeds + 5 pistachios

Dinner: 1–2 bowls cooked sprouts with lots of added vegetables

Before sleeping: 1 glass water with 1 tsp raw unfiltered ACV

THE LIFESTYLE DIET PLAN NO. 40

(Routine diet plan)

Upon waking up: 1 glass water (normal temp) with 1 tsp ACV + 1 tsp haldi

Breakfast: lemon/ginger/tulsi tea + 1–2 moong dal chilla with any homemade chutney + 5 almonds + 5 walnuts

Mid-morning snack: 1 glass orange juice + 1 tbsp sabza seeds

Lunch: 1–2 pieces of grilled fish + homemade solkadi (1 glass) + raw salad on the side

Mid-afternoon snack: 1 cup black coffee with 1 tsp coconut oil + 1 bowl mixed seeds

Dinner: 1 bowl grilled or sautéed mushrooms with sweet potatoes on the side/1 bowl sambar with veggies/1 bowl chana bhel

Before sleeping: 1 glass water with 1 tsp ACV

THE LIFESTYLE DIET PLAN NO. 41

(Routine plan)

Upon waking up: 1 glass water (normal temp) with 1 tsp ACV

Breakfast: lemon/ginger/tulsi tea + 1–2 moong dal chilla + 5 almonds + 5 walnuts

Mid-morning snack: 1 glass orange juice with sabza seeds

Lunch: vegetables salad with mushrooms + homemade buttermilk (1 glass)

Mid-afternoon snack: 1 cup black coffee with coconut oil + 1 bowl mixed seeds

Dinner: 1 bowl homemade tomato/mushroom soup + 1 bowl cooked sprouts/grilled fish with lots of added vegetables on the side

Before sleeping: 1 glass water with 1 tsp ACV

THE LIFESTYLE DIET PLAN NO. 42

(Routine diet plan)

Upon waking up: 1 glass water (normal temp) with 1 tsp ACV

Breakfast: lemon/ginger/tulsi tea + 2 whole eggs or moong dal chilla with chutney + 5 almonds + 5 walnuts

Mid-morning snack: 1 glass carrot + cucumber juice with sabza seeds

Lunch: quinoa upma or rice + 1 bowl grilled fish or chicken or mutton + 1 bowl of any green leafy vegetable + raw salad on the side

Mid-afternoon snack: 1 cup black coffee with coconut oil + 1 bowl mixed seeds + 1 small piece of dark chocolate

Dinner: 1 bowl homemade pumpkin or mushroom soup + 1 bowl cooked sprouts/dal with lots of added vegetables or sweet potatoes on the side

Before sleeping: 1 glass water with 1 tsp ACV

LIFESTYLE DIET PLAN NO. 43

(Diet plan for Diwali [or any festival])

Upon waking up: 1 glass barley water with 1 tsp ACV + 1 tsp turmeric + 5 soaked almonds + 5 soaked walnuts

Breakfast: 2 eggs omelette cooked in ghee + 1 bowl of any seasonal fresh fruit

Mid-morning snack: 1 glass celery juice with lemon and black pepper or Diwali snacks or sweets

Lunch: 1 bowl asparagus/spinach and broccoli/tomato soup + 1 bowl grilled tofu/paneer/fish + raw cucumber, carrot, radish, tomato and onion on the side

Mid-evening snack: 1 small bowl mixed seeds (pumpkin, flax, sunflower, chia, watermelon) + 1 cup coconut coffee

Dinner: 1 bowl cooked sprouts (moong/matki/chavali/black chana) salad with mushrooms and lots of sautéed veggies

Before sleeping: 1 glass barley water with 1 tsp ACV

THE LIFESTYLE DIET PLAN NO. 44

(Super detox and cleanse [intermittent fasting + smoothie cleanse])

Upon waking up: 1 tsp turmeric + ½ tsp ACV in normal water

12:00 p.m. (breakfast): 1 glass morning smoothie (1 bowl spinach + banana + almond milk + 1 tbsp pumpkin and sunflower seeds + 1 tsp cinnamon powder)

1:30 p.m. (mid-morning snack): 1 cup green tea with lemon

3:00 p.m. (lunch): smoothie with mixed dry fruits + apple+ half carrot + pineapple + 1 tbsp homemade dahi + 1 tsp cinnamon powder

5:00 p.m. (mid-evening snack): pomegranate sabza juice (pomegranate + chia seeds + sabza seeds (soaked in water) + sunflower seeds + flax seeds + pumpkin seeds + black or Himalayan salt + lemon)

7:00 p.m.; 3–4 hours before sleeping (dinner): smoothie with berries or green apple + pistachios + 9 almonds + 1 tbsp dahi + some water

THE LIFESTYLE DIET PLAN NO. 45

(Routine diet plan)

Upon waking up: 1 glass fresh wheatgrass juice with 1 tsp raw unfiltered ACV and ½ tsp turmeric

Before workout: 5 soaked almonds + 5 walnuts + 3 apricots + 1 fig

Morning workout and yoga

Breakfast: smoothie with carrots + cucumber + green apple + spinach + ½ avocado + chia and sabza seeds

or

2 eggs bhurji cooked in ghee (1 tbsp)

Mid-morning snack: 1 small bowl roasted makhana + 1 cup green tea with lemon and a pinch of cinnamon powder (home-ground)

Lunch: 1 moong dal chilla (thalipith) + cooked vegetables (all seasonal) + 1 bowl dal

Evening snack: 1 cup black coffee with 1 tbsp coconut oil + 1 bowl roasted mixed seeds (sunflower, pumpkin, flax, chia)

Dinner: tomato/cauliflower/red pumpkin soup + cooked kidney beans salad (kidney beans + cherry tomatoes + bell peppers + broccoli); cook it well and squeeze lemon juice on top

Before sleeping: ½ tbsp raw unfiltered ACV in water

THE LIFESTYLE DIET PLAN NO. 46

(Routine diet plan)

Upon waking up: 1 glass barley water with ½ lemon + 1 tsp turmeric + morning smoothie

Morning walk for 60 min

Breakfast: 1–2 ragi dosas or uttapam with pudina chutney or 1 whole egg omelette (3 times a week)

Mid-morning snack: 1 glass celery juice with lemon and black pepper

Lunch: 1 phulka (khapali gehu)/small jowar bhakri + 1 bowl dal + 1 bowl of any green leafy vegetable + raw onion, tomato, cucumber and radish

Mid-evening snack: 1 bowl mixed seeds + 1 cup black coffee with coconut oil (1 tsp)

Dinner: 1 bowl asparagus/spinach and broccoli/tomato/red pumpkin soup + 1 bowl millet upma with lots of vegetables

Before sleeping: 1 glass barley water with lemon

THE LIFESTYLE DIET PLAN NO. 47

(Diet for Indian fasts)

Upon waking up: 1 glass normal water with 1 tsp ACV and ½ tsp organic turmeric

Breakfast: smoothie with 1 apple + 1 banana + 7–8 almonds + 6 walnut halves + 1 bowl fresh coconut malai + water as per required consistency

Mid-morning snack: 1 glass buttermilk with a pinch of jeera powder and rock salt

Lunch: 1–2 shingada thalipith + 1 bowl peanut curry + roasted sweet potatoes on the side

Mid-evening snack: 1 cup black coffee with 1 tbsp cold-pressed coconut oil + roasted makhana

Dinner; before 7:30 p.m.: 1 small bhakri + 1 bowl of any green leafy vegetable + 1 bowl dal + raw onion, tomato and radish on the side

Post-dinner walk: 60 min

Before sleeping: 1 glass normal water with 1 tsp raw unfiltered ACV

THE LIFESTYLE DIET PLAN NO. 48

(Routine diet plan)

Upon waking up: 1 glass water with ½ lemon + ½ tsp cinnamon powder + ½ tsp turmeric

Before morning walk: green juice with baby spinach + celery + betel leaf + apple + wheatgrass + amla juice + some water

Morning walk and yoga; meditation

Breakfast: moong dal chilla/moong water/dosa/idli with green chutney + 1 cup tea without sugar

Mid-morning snack: 4 almonds + 2 walnuts + 1 fig/coconut water/1 cup green tea

Lunch: 1 bhakri (jowar/bajra/ragi) + 1 bowl any sprouts or pulses sabzi + 1 bowl dal

Evening snacks: 1 cup makhana chivda/1 fruit/1 bowl matki/makhana/murmura (puffed rice) bhel

Dinner: 1 ragi roti frankie/2 idlis with green chutney/1–2 thalipith or dosas or thepla with green chutney

THE LIFESTYLE DIET PLAN NO. 49

(Smoothie detox)

Upon waking up: 1 glass normal water + 1 tsp ACV + 1 tsp turmeric

Breakfast: 1 glass morning smoothie made with handful berries + ½ or 1 banana + ½ cup almond milk + 1 bowl baby spinach + 1 tbsp pumpkin seeds + 1 tsp cinnamon powder

Mid-morning snack: 1 cup green tea with lemon + 1 bowl mixed seeds and nuts

or

1 glass radish juice

Lunch: smoothie made with 1 tbsp mixed nuts + 1 apple + ½ banana + ½ tsp spirulina powder (or consume 1 spirulina tablet) + 1 tbsp sunflower seeds + 1 cup homemade dahi + 1 tsp cinnamon powder

Mid-evening snack: Detox juice with ½ bowl pomegranate + 1 tsp chia seeds + 1 tsp sunflower seeds + 1 tsp flax seeds + 1 tsp pumpkin seeds + black or Himalayan salt + lemon

Dinner (3–4 hours before sleeping): dinner smoothie made with ½ bowl spinach + 1–2 celery sticks + 5–6 pistachios + 7–8 almonds + 1 tsp pumpkin seeds + 1 tbsp dahi + some water as per required consistency

Before sleeping: 1 tsp of ACV in normal water

Snacking options:

1. 1 bowl roasted makhana with rock salt or black salt
2. Sweet potatoes roasted in 1 tsp ghee and turmeric
3. All dry fruits and nuts

THE LIFESTYLE DIET PLAN NO. 50

(Routine diet plan)

Upon waking up: 1 tsp turmeric + ½ tsp ACV in normal water

Breakfast: 1 glass morning smoothie made with berries + avocado + banana + cocoa powder + almond milk + pumpkin seeds + 1 tsp cinnamon powder

or

1 egg and banana pancake

Mid-morning snack: 1 bowl mixed seeds + 1 cup green tea with lemon

Lunch: 1 bhakri (jowar or ragi) or 1 bowl brown rice + 1 bowl chicken or fish curry + raw onion, cucumber, carrot and radish on the side

Mid-evening snack: 1 cup black coffee with coconut oil (1 tsp) + 8 roasted almonds

Dinner (3–4 hours before sleeping): dinner smoothie with mixed dry fruits + apple + avocado + pineapple + 1 bowl spinach and salad leaves + 1 tbsp homemade dahi + 1 tsp cinnamon powder

THE LIFESTYLE DIET PLAN NO. 51

(Partial smoothie detox)

Upon waking up: 1 tsp turmeric + ½ tsp ACV in normal water

Breakfast: 1 glass morning smoothie with berries + ½ avocado + spinach + carrots + banana + almond milk + pumpkin seeds + 1 tsp cinnamon powder

Mid-morning snack: 1 glass buttermilk

Lunch: 1 bowl chicken or fish salad with kefir and lime

Mid-evening snack: 1 bowl homemade matki bhel with a little tamarind water + 1 cup green tea with lemon

Dinner (3–4 hours before sleeping): dinner smoothie made with ½ green apple or kiwi + pistachios + 8–9 almonds + avocado + 1 tbsp dahi + some water according to required consistency

or

1–2 bowls of any homemade soup (vegetable soup)

THE LIFESTYLE DIET PLAN NO. 52

(Routine diet plan)

Upon waking up: 1 tsp turmeric + ½ tsp ACV in normal water

Breakfast: 1 glass morning smoothie with ½ apple + banana + spinach + 8 almonds + 1 tbsp dahi + pumpkin seeds + 1 tsp cinnamon powder

or

2 eggs bhurji cooked in ghee

Mid-morning snack: 1 bowl mixed seeds + 1 cup green tea with lemon

Lunch: 1 bhakri (jowar or ragi) or 1 bowl brown rice + 1 bowl chicken or fish curry + raw onion, cucumber, carrot and radish on the side

Mid-evening snack: 1 cup black coffee with coconut oil (1 tsp) + 8 roasted almonds

Dinner (3–4 hours before sleeping): dinner smoothie made with mixed dry fruits + 1 apple + ½ bowl moong sprouts + 1 bowl spinach and salad leaves + 1 tbsp homemade dahi + 1 tsp cinnamon powder

THE LIFESTYLE DIET PLAN NO. 53

(Diet for strength, energy and weight gain)

Upon waking up: 1 glass fresh lemon water + 1 tsp turmeric

Pre-training snack: 1 banana + 1 bowl mixed dry fruits

Morning workout session

Immediately after training: 1 scoop of any plant-based protein powder in warm water + 1 tsp coconut oil

Breakfast: 1–2 bowls daliya + 2–3 eggs omelette/boiled + 1 B-complex capsule

Mid-morning snack: 1 cup green tea with lemon + 1 fruit (any seasonal)

Lunch: 1–2 bowls soaked brown or red rice + 1–2 bowls chicken curry (coconut-based) + raw onion, radish and tomato

Mid-evening snack: smoothie: green smoothie made with banana + yoghurt + spinach + mixed seeds + dates + apple + any other vegetable

6:45 p.m.: 1 bowl of dahi with mixed dry fruits

8:30 p.m. (dinner): 1–2 ragi rotis + black or yellow dal + 3 boiled eggs (with yolk) + roasted sweet potatoes on the sides + raw onion, tomato and radish

THE LIFESTYLE DIET PLAN NO. 54

(Routine diet plan)

Upon waking up: 1 glass water with ½ tsp ACV + 1 tsp turmeric

Morning walk or workout for 60 min

Breakfast: 2 eggs bhurji or omelette with 1 cup green tea with lemon

Mid-morning snack: 1 glass celery juice with lemon and black pepper

Lunch: 1 small jowar bhakri + 1 bowl dal + 1 bowl of any green leafy vegetable + raw onion, tomato, cucumber and radish

Mid-evening snack: 1 bowl mixed seeds + 1 cup black coffee with coconut oil (1 tsp)

Dinner: 1 bowl asparagus/spinach and broccoli/tomato/red pumpkin soup + 1 bowl grilled mushrooms + lots of vegetables and roasted sweet potatoes on the side

Before sleeping: 1 glass water with lemon

THE LIFESTYLE DIET PLAN NO. 55

(Diet plan for weight gain)

Upon waking up: 1 glass normal water with ½ lemon and 1 tsp turmeric

20 min after waking up: overnight soaked 5 almonds + 5 walnuts + 3 dried figs + 2 dates

Breakfast: 1–2 thalipith (paratha) with pudina chutney or idli/dosa/uttapam with sambar and coconut chutney

Mid-morning snack: 1 fresh fruit (any seasonal) or 1 dry fruits ladoo or dinkacha (gond) ladoo

Lunch: 2 khapali gehu roti or ragi or bajra roti + 1 bowl of any green leafy vegetable + 1 bowl dal with rice and 1 tsp ghee + koshimbir (raita) or salad on the side

Evening snack: 1 glass fresh pomegranate juice + 1 bowl roasted seeds (pumpkin, flax, sunflower and chia)

Dinner: 1 bowl moong dal khichadi + 1 tsp ghee + 1 bowl any seasonal vegetables

or

2 phulkas (khapali gehu) + 1 bowl of any green leafy vegetable + 1 bowl dal with rice and 1 tsp ghee + koshimbir or salad on the side

THE LIFESTYLE DIET PLAN NO. 56

(Diet plan for kids)

Morning snack (before school): 1–2 dry fruits ladoo (ingredients of ladoo: almonds, walnuts, cashews, pistachios, figs, dates, jaggery, coconut, ghee) with 1 glass milk (with 1 scoop kids protein since kids need a quick high-protein morning meal before school)

or

Omelette or French toast cooked in ghee

Lunch: mixed veggies frankie in ragi roti or white rice with sprouts and vegetables or homemade sourdough bread sandwiches + 1 seasonal fruit

After school: 1 fruit (any seasonal) and 1 dinkacha ladoo

Evening snacks: 1–2 vegetable paratha or thalipith with chutney or idli/dosa/uttapam with coconut chutney or chapati roll with different vegetable stuffing

Dinner: 1–2 roti (khapali gehu/jowar/bajra) + 1 bowl of any green leafy vegetable + 1 bowl dal with rice and 1 tsp ghee + koshimbir or salad on the side

THE LIFESTYLE DIET PLAN NO. 57

(Intermittent fasting)

Morning pre- or post-workout snack: 1 cup black coffee with 1 tbsp ghee or coconut oil

2:00 p.m.: morning drink of 1 glass barley water with 1 tsp raw unfiltered ACV and ½ tsp turmeric

2:15 p.m. (lunch): 1 bowl cooked sprouts with tomatoes, onions, cucumber, a pinch of rock salt, black pepper and lemon juice

or

2 moong dal chilla with coconut chutney

4:00 p.m. (mid-evening snack): 1 bowl mixed seeds + 5 almonds + 5 walnuts + 1 fig

6:00 p.m. (dinner): 1 bowl quinoa rice + 1 bowl cooked vegetables (all seasonal) + 1 bowl dal + raw onion, tomato, radish and cucumber on the side

Before sleeping: 1 glass barley water

THE LIFESTYLE DIET PLAN NO. 58

(Smoothie detox)

Upon waking up: 1 tsp turmeric + ½ tsp ACV in normal water

20 min before breakfast: 1 cup black coffee with 1 tsp ghee or coconut oil

Breakfast: 1 glass morning smoothie made with strawberries + spinach + avocado + banana + almond milk + pumpkin seeds + 1 tsp cinnamon powder

Mid-morning snack: 8 almonds + 5 walnuts + 1 cup green tea with lemon

Lunch: smoothie made with mixed dry fruits + apple + avocado + kiwi + 1 bowl spinach and salad leaves + 1 tbsp homemade dahi + 1 tsp cinnamon powder

Mid-evening snack: 1 bowl roasted makhana chivda with 1 cup herbal tea

Dinner: smoothie made with ½ green apple + pistachios + avocado + 1 tbsp dahi + some water as per required consistency

THE LIFESTYLE DIET PLAN NO. 59

(Routine diet plan)

Upon waking up: 1 glass water with ½ tsp ACV + 1 tsp turmeric

Morning walk or workout for 60 min

Breakfast: 1–2 ragi dosas or uttapam with pudina chutney or 2 egg omelettes

Mid-morning snack: 1 bowl freshly cut avocado or fresh coconut chunks with 1 tbsp soaked sabza seeds

Lunch: 1 jowar/ragi bhakri + 1 bowl dal + 1 bowl of any green leafy vegetable + raw onion, tomato, cucumber and radish

Mid-evening snack: 1 bowl mixed seeds + 1 cup black coffee with coconut oil (1 tsp)

Dinner: 1 bowl asparagus/spinach and broccoli/cauliflower/tomato/red pumpkin soup + 1 bowl grilled chicken or fish with lots of vegetables

Before sleeping: 1 glass water with lemon

THE LIFESTYLE DIET PLAN NO. 60

(Intermittent fasting)

10:00 a.m.: Morning drink with 1 tsp turmeric + ½ tsp ACV in barley water or plain water

10:15 a.m. (breakfast): 1 moong dal chilla with pudina chutney

or

2 whole eggs bhurji or omelette

Mid-morning snack: 1 glass carrot and cucumber juice with ½ lemon and sabza seeds

2:30 p.m. (lunch): 1 bhakri (jowar/ragi) + 1 bowl of any green leafy vegetable + 1 bowl dal + raw salad or koshimbir on the side

Mid-evening snack: 1 bowl mixed seeds + 6 almonds + 1 cup green tea with lemon

6:00 p.m. (dinner): 1 bowl homemade cauliflower/mushroom/tomato/red pumpkin/sweet potato soup + cooked sprouts (moong/matki/chavali/masoor) + 1 bowl koshimbir (any of your choice)

THE LIFESTYLE DIET PLAN NO. 61

(Intermittent fasting)

Upon waking up: 1 tsp turmeric + ½ tsp ACV in normal water

10:00 a.m. (breakfast): 1 cup butter coffee (blend black coffee + 1 tsp ghee or 1 tsp coconut oil) + 5 almonds + 5 walnuts (soaked overnight in water)

1:30 p.m. (lunch): 1 bowl grilled chicken or fish (with your choice of marination) with baby spinach + chopped beetroot + carrots + cucumbers + any cheese of your choice + 1 tbsp balsamic vinegar + handful berries

Mid-evening snack: 1 cup herbal tea with lots of ginger + 1 tsp turmeric and ½ lemon

5:30 p.m. (dinner; 3–4 hours before sleeping): ragi or jowar wrap with chicken keema/hummus/eggs filling with sweet potatoes, tomatoes, mixed veggies with rock salt and pepper

THE LIFESTYLE DIET PLAN NO. 62

(Routine diet plan)

Upon waking up: 1 tsp turmeric + ½ tsp ACV in normal water

Before workout: 1 cup butter coffee (freshly brewed black coffee + 1 tsp cow ghee + 1 spoon collagen powder)

Breakfast: 1 glass morning smoothie made with berries + avocado + banana+ cocoa powder + almond milk + pumpkin seeds + 1 tsp cinnamon powder

Mid-morning snack: 1 bowl mixed seeds + 1 cup green tea with lemon

Lunch: 1 bowl sprouted moong salad with cooked broccoli and zucchini + ½ avocado on the side

or

1 ragi bhakri with 1 bowl vegetable and dal

Mid-evening snack: 1 cup green tea with a pinch of cinnamon powder and lemon + 8 roasted almonds

Dinner (3–4 hours before sleeping): dinner smoothie made with mixed dry fruits + apple + avocado + pineapple + 1 bowl spinach and salad leaves + 1 tbsp homemade dahi + 1 tsp cinnamon powder

THE LIFESTYLE DIET PLAN NO. 63

(Intermittent fasting)

Upon waking up: 1 tsp turmeric + ½ tsp ACV in normal water

10:00 a.m. (breakfast): 1 cup butter coffee (blend black coffee + 1 tsp ghee + 1 scoop collagen powder) + 5 almonds + 5 walnuts (soaked overnight in water)

1:30 p.m. (lunch): 1 jowar or ragi bhakri/1 bowl brown rice + 1 bowl chicken or fish curry + 1 bowl koshimbir on the side (with carrots, cucumber and dahi)

Mid-evening snack: 1 cup herbal tea with lots of ginger, 1 tsp turmeric and ½ lemon

5:30 p.m. (dinner; 3–4 hours before sleeping): smoothie made with 1 bowl carrots + ½ banana + ½ avocado + ½ apple + 1 bowl baby spinach + 1 tbsp mixed seeds + 7–8 almonds

THE LIFESTYLE DIET PLAN NO. 64

(Routine diet plan)

Upon waking up: 1 cup water (normal temp) + raw unfiltered ACV + 1 tsp turmeric

Before workout: 1 cup butter coffee (freshly brewed black coffee + 1 tsp cold-pressed coconut oil + 1 scoop collagen powder, all to be blended together for 20 sec)

Breakfast: lemon/ginger/tulsi tea + 1–2 homemade thalipith (with vegetables) and chutney

or

2 eggs bhurji

or

1 bowl ragi porridge with chia seeds on top

Mid-morning snack: 1 glass super green smoothie made with spinach + curry leaves + betel leaf + ½ avocado + 1 tbsp pumpkin seeds + sabza seeds

Lunch: 1 bhakri or 1 bowl brown rice + 1 bowl dal/chicken/fish + raw tomato, onion, radish and carrot on the side

Evening snacks: 1 cup green tea with 7 almonds + 5 walnuts + mixed seeds

Dinner (7:30 p.m.): 1 bowl red pumpkin or broccoli or sweet potato soup + 1 bowl cooked sprouted moong/matki/chavali/green peas sautéed with vegetables

Before sleeping: 1 glass water with raw unfiltered ACV

THE LIFESTYLE DIET PLAN NO. 65

(Detox diet plan)

Upon waking up: 1 cup water (normal temp) with wheatgrass juice and lemon + 1 Vibact DS capsule

Breakfast: lemon/ginger/tulsi tea + 1 bowl cooked sprouted moong with tomato, onion and lemon juice

Mid-morning snack: 1 glass celery juice with lemon and a pinch of black pepper

Lunch: steamed vegetables (cauliflower, broccoli, spinach, bell peppers) with sautéed mushrooms + homemade buttermilk (1–2 glasses)

Mid-afternoon snack: any 1 seasonal fruit + 7 almonds + 4 walnut halves + 1 cup green tea with lemon

Dinner: pumpkin/sweet potatoes/carrots and zucchini soup + sprouts usal (any; 1 bowl) with pickles (homemade)

Before sleeping: 1 glass water with 1 tsp raw unfiltered ACV

THE LIFESTYLE DIET PLAN NO. 66

(Routine diet plan)

Morning drink: 1 glass water (lukewarm) with lemon + green juice made with wheatgrass + betel leaf + spinach + basil leaves + mint leaves + celery or coriander leaves + ½ tsp turmeric + a pinch of black pepper and cinnamon powder + ½ lemon

Morning walk or yoga

Breakfast: moong dal chilla with pudina chutney or homemade idli/dosa/uttapam with coconut chutney

or

Overnight soaked oats with dahi, dry fruits, sabza seeds and banana

or

1 bowl nachni porridge

or

1 bowl daliya

Mid-morning snack: 1 glass juice made with carrots + cucumber + ½ radish + ½ orange + 1 tsp sabza seeds

Lunch: ragi roti/bhakri + 1 bowl cooked vegetable (any seasonal) + 1 bowl dal (black or yellow) + raita on the side

Mid-evening snack: 1 bowl roasted makhana or 1 homemade ladoo (made with edible gum, dry fruits, seeds, coconut and ghee) + 1 cup green tea with lemon

Dinner: pumpkin/sweet potatoes/carrots and zucchini soup + sprouts usal (any; 1 bowl) with pickles (homemade)

or

1–2 bowls soup made with sautéed vegetables with mushrooms

or

1 bowl soup with homemade Thai curry and brown rice

Before sleeping: 1 glass normal water + ½ tsp raw unfiltered ACV + 1 Econorm sachet

THE LIFESTYLE DIET PLAN NO. 67

(Routine diet plan)

Upon waking up: 1 cup water (normal temp) with raw unfiltered ACV + 1 tsp turmeric

Before workout: 1 cup black coffee + 1 tsp coconut oil (raw, unfiltered) + 5 almonds + 5 walnuts

Breakfast: lemon/ginger/tulsi tea + 2 eggs bhurji cooked in ghee or 1 thalipith or paratha (use any vegetable stuffing) with pudina chutney

Mid-morning snack: 1 glass super green smoothie made with spinach + curry leaves + betel leaf + ½ avocado + 1 tbsp pumpkin seeds + sabza seeds

Lunch: 1 bowl cooked sprouted moong/matki/chavali/green peas with sautéed vegetables + homemade raita or koshimbir on the side

Evening snacks: 1 cup green tea with lemon + 1 bowl mixed seeds (pumpkin, flax, chia and sunflower)

Dinner (7:30 p.m.): 1 bowl red pumpkin or green peas or broccoli or sweet potato soup + 1 bowl grilled chicken or fish or mushrooms with sauteed veggies

Before sleeping: 1 glass water with raw unfiltered ACV

THE LIFESTYLE DIET PLAN NO. 68

(Routine diet plan)

Upon waking up: 1 cup water (normal temp) + wheatgrass juice + ½ tsp ACV and turmeric

20 min before breakfast: 1 glass black coffee or warm water + 1 tsp coconut oil

Breakfast: 2 eggs bhurji

or

1–2 thalipith with vegetable stuffing + 1 bowl pudina chutney

Mid-morning snack: 1 glass juice made with carrots + cucumber + orange with sabza seeds and a pinch of black pepper

Lunch: steamed vegetables (cauliflower, broccoli, spinach, bell peppers) with sautéed mushrooms + homemade buttermilk (1–2 glasses)

Mid-afternoon snack: 1 bowl papaya or strawberries + 7 almonds + 4 walnut halves + 1 cup green tea with lemon

Dinner: red pumpkin/sweet potatoes/carrots soup + sprouts usal (any; 1 bowl) with pickles (homemade)

Before sleeping: 1 glass water with 1 tsp raw unfiltered ACV

THE LIFESTYLE DIET PLAN NO. 69

(Detox diet plan)

Upon waking up: 1 cup water (normal temp) with wheatgrass powder and lemon

Breakfast: lemon/ginger/tulsi tea + 1 bowl cooked sprouted moong with tomatoes, onions and lemon juice

Mid-morning snack: 1 bowl any seasonal fruit + 5 walnuts + 1 tab Celin (vitamin C) + 1 capsule Vibact DS (probiotic)

Lunch: vegetables salad with mushrooms + homemade buttermilk (1–2 glasses)

Mid-afternoon snack: 1 bowl papaya + 7 almonds + 4 walnuts

Dinner: boiled vegetable soup + usal (any; 1 bowl) with roasted sweet potatoes

Before sleeping: 1 glass water with 1 tsp Triphala churna

THE LIFESTYLE DIET PLAN NO. 70

(Intermittent fasting gut healing diet)

10:00 a.m.: morning drink (on an empty stomach) consisting of 50 ml fresh wheatgrass juice (add 50 ml of water) + 1 tsp raw unfiltered ACV + ½ tsp turmeric + 1 Econorm sachet (add to the wheatgrass drink itself) + zinc

Before workout: 1 cup black coffee + 1 tsp cow ghee

Morning workout

Breakfast: smoothie made with carrots + cucumber + green apple + spinach + ½ avocado + 1 scoop collagen powder + spirulina powder + chia and sabza seeds

or

2 eggs bhurji cooked in ghee + 1 cup bone broth (instead of collagen) + supplements of vitamin B5, magnesium and probiotic

Lunch: 1 moong dal chilla (thalipith) + cooked vegetables (all seasonal) + 1 bowl dal + raw salad on the side

5:00 p.m. (evening snacks): 1 bowl roasted mixed seeds (sunflower, pumpkin, flax, chia) + 1 cup green tea or herbal tea (ginger + lemongrass + basil leaves + turmeric + ajwain and some lemon)

7:30 p.m. (dinner): tomato/cauliflower/red pumpkin/sweet potato soup + cooked kidney beans or moong salad (sprouted kidney beans or moong + cherry tomatoes + bell peppers +

green peas + broccoli); cook this well and add lemon juice on top + roasted sweet potatoes in ghee (with a pinch of sea salt and turmeric) on the side (optional)

Fasting window begins: Hydrate well during the fasting window

THE LIFESTYLE DIET PLAN NO. 71

(Routine diet plan [gut and skin recovery])

Morning drink: 1 tsp turmeric + ½ tsp ACV in barley water or plain water + 1 glass green juice made with spinach + celery + 1 betel leaf + ½ green apple + wheatgrass powder + 1 tsp cinnamon powder + ½ lemon

Breakfast: 1 moong dal chilla with pudina chutney

or

2 eggs bhurji or omelette

Mid-morning snack: 1 glass juice containing carrots + berries + beetroot + ginger + cucumber + ½ orange + sabza seeds

Lunch: 1 bowl quinoa or couscous upma with lots of fresh vegetables + 1 bowl koshimbir or raita or dahi (homemade)

Mid-evening snack: 1 cup black coffee with 1 tsp coconut oil in it + 1 bowl mixed seeds + 6 almonds + 5 walnuts

Dinner: 1 bowl pumpkin or broccoli soup + sautéed mushrooms/fish with roasted sweet potatoes on the side + 1 bowl koshimbir (any of your choice)

Drink warm water between the meals.

Before sleeping: 1 glass warm water + 1 tsp Triphala churna

THE LIFESTYLE DIET PLAN NO. 72

(Intermittent fasting diet plan)

10:00 a.m.: wake up; 1 tsp turmeric + ½ tsp ACV in water

10:15 a.m. (breakfast): smoothie made with strawberries + banana + 8 almonds + 6 walnuts + 1 bowl carrots + 1 tbsp dahi + coconut malai + 1 tbsp pumpkin seeds + 1 tsp chia seeds

11:30 p.m.: 1 glass celery juice or buttermilk

1:00 p.m. (lunch): 1 bowl grilled chicken or fish salad with bell peppers, sweet potatoes, green peas, broccoli and zucchini

5:30 p.m. (evening snack): 1 bowl chana bhel (homemade) + 1 cup green tea

6:00 p.m. (dinner): smoothie made with carrots + cucumber + ½ banana + ½ avocado + ½ apple + 1 bowl baby spinach + 1 tbsp mixed seeds + 7–8 almonds + 4 walnut halves

Before sleeping: 1 glass warm water + 1 tsp Triphala churna

THE LIFESTYLE DIET PLAN NO. 73

(Intermittent fasting [advanced])

Upon waking up: 1 tsp turmeric + ½ tsp ACV in water

1:00 p.m. (lunch): 1 bowl grilled chicken or fish salad with bell peppers, sweet potatoes, green peas, broccoli and zucchini + 1 cup green tea with lemon

5:30 p.m. (evening snack): 1 bowl makhana + 1 cup herbal tea with lemon

8:30 p.m. (dinner): smoothie made with carrots + cucumber + ½ banana + ½ avocado + ½ apple + strawberries + 1 bowl baby spinach + 1 tbsp mixed seeds + 7–8 almonds + 4 walnut halves

Before sleeping: 1 glass warm water with 1 tsp Triphala churna

THE LIFESTYLE DIET PLAN NO. 74

(Intermittent fasting diet)

Upon waking up: 1 glass water with ½ tsp ACV + 1 tsp turmeric

Morning walk or workout for 60 min

2:00 p.m. (breakfast): 2 eggs (omelette or bhurji) + 1 bowl of freshly cut seasonal fruits + 1 glass (celery + spinach) juice with lemon and black pepper

3:30 p.m. (lunch): 1 bowl cooked sprouted moong/matki/chavali/green peas sautéed with vegetables

5:00 p.m. (mid-evening snack): 1 bowl mixed seeds + 1 cup black coffee with coconut oil (1 tsp)

7:00 p.m. (dinner): 1 bowl asparagus/spinach and broccoli/cauliflower/tomato/red pumpkin soup + 1 bowl grilled chicken or fish or paneer or mushrooms with lots of vegetables

Before sleeping: 1 glass warm water with 1 tsp Triphala

THE LIFESTYLE DIET PLAN NO. 75

(Intermittent fasting for fat loss, gut health and recovery)

Morning drink (on an empty stomach): 1 glass water + 1 tsp raw unfiltered ACV + 1 tsp turmeric

Morning workout

Green juice with ½ bowl spinach + 1 tbsp mint leaves + 1 tbsp neem leaves + 1 betel leaf + fresh wheatgrass + few basil leaves + ½ tsp cinnamon powder + a pinch of pink or rock salt + ½ lemon juice + 1 ashwagandha tablet

Breakfast: 1–2 moong dal or urad dal dosas with pudina chutney + 2 eggs omelette or bhurji

Mid-morning snack: 1 cup black coffee + 1 bowl mixed seeds (sunflower, pumpkin, flax, chia)

Lunch: 1 bhakri + 1 bowl of any green leafy vegetable + 1 bowl dal + dahi or koshimbir on the side

Mid-evening snack: 1 cup kombucha tea + 5 almonds + 5 walnut halves + 5 cashews

Dinner (7:00 p.m.): 1 bowl bone broth soup + 200 gm chicken or fish or sprouts + any cooked seasonal vegetable

Follow this up with 16 hours of fasting.

Before sleeping: 1 glass warm water + 1 tsp Triphala

THE LIFESTYLE DIET PLAN NO. 76

(Routine diet plan)

Upon waking up: 1 glass water + ½ tsp ACV + 1 tsp turmeric

1 hour before workout: 5–6 soaked almonds + 5 walnuts + 1 fig

Breakfast: 1 cup butter coffee + some nuts and seeds

Mid-morning snack: 1 glass celery or cucumber juice with lemon and black pepper

Lunch: 1 bowl brown rice or 1 dosa or 1 uttapam + 1 bowl dal or sambar + 1 bowl of any green leafy vegetable + raw onion, tomato, cucumber and radish

Mid-evening snack: 1 bowl mixed seeds + 1 cup herbal tea

Dinner: 1 bowl asparagus/spinach and broccoli/cauliflower/tomato/red pumpkin soup + 1 bowl sautéed mushrooms or dal with lots of vegetables

THE LIFESTYLE DIET PLAN NO. 77

(Routine diet plan for PCOD)

Morning drink: 1 glass of normal water + 1 tsp ACV + 1 tsp haldi + butter coffee (with 1 tbsp ghee or coconut oil)

Breakfast: smoothie made with banana + avocado + 6 almonds + 6 walnuts + 1 tsp flax seeds + 1 tsp chia seeds + water

Lunch: 1–2 moong dal dosas with any vegetable and dal + 1 bowl dahi

Mid-evening snack: 1 cup matcha tea with cinnamon and lemon + 1 bowl soaked mixed seeds

Dinner: 1 bowl cooked sprouts or chicken or fish + 1 bowl cooked vegetables or any soup of your choice + 1 capsule omega + 1 tablet vitex

Before sleeping: 1 glass normal water with 1 tsp ACV

THE LIFESTYLE DIET PLAN NO. 78

(Diet plan for gut healing [for diseases such as IBS/IBD])

Upon waking up: 1 glass fresh aloe vera juice + 1 tbsp L glutamine powder + Enterogermina vial

Breakfast: smoothie made with green apple + banana + sabza seeds + ashwagandha powder + mulethi powder) + 1–2 moong dal or urad dal chilla or dosa/idlis + 5 almonds + 5 walnuts + 1 Primosa capsule

Lunch: 1 nachni/jowar/bajra dosa or bhakri + 1 bowl of any green leafy vegetable + 1 bowl dal + radish koshimbir or dahi on the side

Mid-evening snack: 1 glass aloe vera juice + 1 tbsp L glutamine powder + 1 small bowl mixed seeds

Dinner: 1 bowl asparagus/pumpkin/broccoli/spinach soup + 1 bowl cabbage sabzi or any seasonal vegetables with quinoa upma or rice

Before sleeping: 1 glass aloe vera juice with 1 tsp Triphala powder

THE LIFESTYLE DIET PLAN NO. 79

(Routine diet plan)

Upon waking up: 1 glass fresh wheatgrass juice + 1 tsp raw unfiltered ACV and ½ tsp turmeric

Before workout: 5 soaked almonds + 5 walnuts + 3 apricots + 1 fig

Morning workout and yoga

Breakfast: smoothie with carrots + cucumber + green apple + spinach + ½ avocado + chia and sabza seeds + coconut or almond milk + 1 scoop plant-based protein powder

Lunch: 1 moong dal chilla + cooked vegetables (all seasonal) + 1 bowl dal

Evening snacks: 1 cup black coffee + 1 bowl roasted mixed seeds (sunflower, pumpkin, flax, chia)

Dinner (before 7:30 p.m.): tomato/cauliflower/red pumpkin soup + cooked kidney beans salad (kidney beans + cherry tomatoes + bell peppers + broccoli); cook this well and add lemon juice on top

Before sleeping: 1 glass aloe vera juice + 1 tsp Triphala powder

THE LIFESTYLE DIET PLAN NO. 80

(Routine diet plan)

Morning drink: 1 glass water (lukewarm) with lemon

Breakfast: smoothie made with spinach + banana + apple + 6 almonds + 6 walnuts + flax seeds + 1 tsp sabza seeds + 1 tsp dahi + water

Lunch: moong dal chilla with pudina chutney or homemade idli/dosa/uttapam with coconut chutney

or

1 bowl daliya

Mid-evening snack: 1 cup green tea with lemon

Dinner: any homemade salad with cooked sprouts + 1 cup dahi

Before sleeping: 1 glass aloe vera juice + 1 tsp Triphala powder

THE LIFESTYLE DIET PLAN NO. 81

(Routine diet plan)

Upon waking up: 1 glass water with 1 tsp raw unfiltered ACV + ½ tsp turmeric

Breakfast: 1 bowl overnight soaked oats with fresh fruits, nuts and seeds on top + 1 cup matcha green tea

Mid-morning snack: 1 cup herbal tea with lemon + 6 almonds + 2 walnuts

Lunch: 1 moong dal chilla or dosa or thalipith + cooked vegetables (all seasonal) + 1 bowl dal + koshimbir on the side

Evening snack: 1 glass radish juice

Dinner: tomato/cauliflower/red pumpkin soup + cooked kidney beans salad (kidney beans + cherry tomatoes + bell peppers + broccoli); cook this well and add lemon juice on top

Before sleeping: ½ tsp raw unfiltered ACV with water

THE LIFESTYLE DIET PLAN NO. 82

(Intermittent fasting + gut healing diet plan)

10:30 a.m. (morning drink): 1 glass water with ACV + 1 tsp haldi + 1 Vibact capsule

12:00 p.m.: 1 glass smoothie (carrots + cucumber + strawberries + banana + 8 almonds + 1 tsp mixed seeds)

or

2–3 eggs bhurji

or

chocolate oats smoothie (1 banana + ½ apple + raw cacao powder + 2 tbsp overnight soaked oats + 8 almonds or mixed nuts + 1 tbsp pumpkin seeds+ 1 tbsp dahi) + collagen powder + 2 ashwagandha tablets + 1 cap osmega + 1 tab B long F

Mid-morning snack: 1 cup black coffee with 1 tsp coconut oil

2:30 p.m. (lunch): 1 bowl dal + 1 bowl of any cooked vegetable or usal + 1 bowl raita or koshimbir

Mid-evening snack: 1 bowl mixed seeds + 6 almonds + 1 cup green tea with lemon

20 min before dinner: 1 tsp coconut oil in warm water

7:00 p.m. to 7:30 p.m. (dinner): 1 bowl homemade cauliflower/ mushroom soup/tomato/red pumpkin/sweet potatoes soup + cooked sprouts (moong/matki/chavali/masoor) + 1 bowl koshimbir (any of your choice)

or

any homemade soup + 1 bowl grilled chicken or fish

or

1–2 thalipith with chutney or cooked vegetables

or

Homemade dosa or idlis with coconut chutney and sambar

Before sleeping: 1 glass water with 1 tsp raw unfiltered ACV + 2 tablets of Triphala

Tip: Try to finish dinner by 7:00 or 7:30 p.m.

THE LIFESTYLE DIET PLAN NO. 83

(Diet plan for Indian fasts)

Wake up: 1 glass normal water with 1 tsp ACV and ½ tsp organic turmeric

Breakfast: 1 glass buttermilk + 1 peanut and jaggery ladoo

Lunch: 1–2 shingada (kuttu or amaranth flour) thalipith + 1 bowl peanut curry + roasted sweet potatoes on the side

Mid-evening snack: 1 cup black coffee with 1 tbsp cold-pressed coconut oil + roasted makhana

Dinner: smoothie made with ½ green apple + pistachios + avocado + 1 tbsp dahi + some water as per the required consistency

Post-dinner walk: 60 min

Before sleeping: 1 glass normal water with 1 tsp raw unfiltered ACV

THE LIFESTYLE DIET PLAN NO. 84

(Intermittent fasting diet plan)

Upon waking up: 1 tsp turmeric + ½ tsp ACV in normal water

20 min before breakfast: 1 cup black coffee with 1 tsp ghee or coconut oil

1:00 p.m. (breakfast): 3 eggs bhurji or omelette or boiled eggs

2:30 p.m. (lunch): 1 millet roti + 1 bowl dal + 1 bowl of any sabzi + 1 bowl koshimbir

5:00 p.m. (mid-evening snack): 1 bowl green tea with lemon or black coffee with coconut oil + 1 bowl mixed nuts and mixed seeds

8:00 p.m. (dinner; 3–4 hours before sleeping): 1–2 bowls of sautéed vegetables + 1 bowl chicken or fish

Before sleeping: 1 glass normal water with 1 tsp raw unfiltered ACV

THE LIFESTYLE DIET PLAN NO. 85

(Routine diet plan for hormonal balance)

Upon waking up: 1 glass water with 1 tsp raw unfiltered ACV and ½ tsp turmeric

Breakfast: 1 cup ghee coffee (add 1 tbsp cow ghee to black coffee and blend until it is frothy) + 7–8 almonds

Mid-morning snack: 1 small bowl roasted makhana or 1 avocado + 1 cup green tea with lemon with a pinch of cinnamon powder (home-ground)

Lunch: 1–2 buckwheat or amaranth paratha + cooked vegetables (all seasonal) + 1 bowl dal or 2 eggs bhurji

Evening snack: 1 cup black coffee with 1 tsp coconut oil + 1 bowl roasted mixed seeds (sunflower, pumpkin, flax, chia)

Dinner (4–5 hours before sleeping): 1–2 moong dosas or chilla with sabzi and dal + 1 bowl raita (any homemade raita without sugar)

Before sleeping: 1 glass warm water with 1 tsp Triphala

THE LIFESTYLE DIET PLAN NO. 86

(Routine diet plan for gut healing)

Upon waking up: 1 tsp turmeric + ½ tsp ACV in normal water + Vibact

Breakfast: 1 cup coconut coffee + 8 soaked almonds

Mid-morning snack: 1 glass plain lemon water (1 whole lemon) with L glutamine + collagen powder + zinc + magnesium

Lunch: 1 bowl quinoa (soaked for at least 4–5 hours) rice with any cooked vegetable + 1 bowl raita

Mid-evening snack: 1 avocado with 2–3 strawberries + 1 cup herbal tea

Dinner (3–4 hours before sleeping): 1 bowl red/black rice with mushroom/moong/broccoli/plain dal/Thai curry + raita on the side

Before sleeping: 1 glass warm with 1 tsp Triphala

THE LIFESTYLE DIET PLAN NO. 87

(Routine diet plan)

Upon waking up: 1 glass water with ½ tsp ACV + 1 tsp turmeric

Morning walk or workout for 60 min

Breakfast: 1 cup ghee coffee + 2 eggs omelette

Mid-morning snack: 7 almonds + 2 walnuts + 1 fig

Lunch: 1 jowar/ragi bhakri + 1 bowl dal + 1 bowl of any green leafy or any seasonal vegetable + raw onion, tomato, cucumber and radish

Mid-evening snack: 1 bowl mixed seeds + 1 cup black coffee with coconut oil

Dinner: 1 bowl of any homemade dal + 1 bowl of any homemade cooked vegetable + 1 glass buttermilk

Before sleeping: 1 glass water with 1 tsp Triphala

THE LIFESTYLE DIET PLAN NO. 88

(Routine diet plan)

Upon waking up: 1 tsp turmeric + ½ tsp ACV in normal water + Vibact

Before workout: 1 cup coconut coffee

Breakfast: 2 eggs bhurji + 1 bowl of any seasonal fruit

Mid-morning snack: 1 cup green tea with lemon + 1 bowl mixed seeds

Lunch: 1 moong dal chilla or thalipith or dosa + cooked vegetables (any seasonal) + 1 bowl dal or sprouts curry + koshimbir or raita on the side

Mid-evening snack: 1 bowl mixed seeds with 1 cup herbal tea (ginger, tulsi, cinnamon, lemongrass, ajwain and saunf)

Dinners (7:30 p.m.): tomato/cauliflower/red pumpkin soup + cooked kidney beans or grilled chicken or fish or chickpeas salad (cherry tomatoes + bell peppers + broccoli); cook this well and add lemon juice on top

Before sleeping: 1 tsp raw unfiltered ACV in normal water

THE LIFESTYLE DIET PLAN NO. 89

(Routine diet plan)

Upon waking up: 1 glass water with 1 tsp raw unfiltered ACV and ½ tsp turmeric

After workout: butter coffee (alternate with ghee or coconut oil)

Breakfast: 2 eggs omelette + ½ avocado + 2 ashwagandha tablets

Mid-morning snack: 1 glass celery juice or carrot and cucumber juice with sabza seeds, black pepper and lemon

Lunch: 1 moong dal chilla or dosa + cooked vegetables (all seasonal) + 1 glass buttermilk

Evening snack: 1 bowl roasted mixed seeds (sunflower, pumpkin, flax, chia) + 1 cup herbal tea with lemon

Dinner (before 7:30 p.m.): 1 bowl of any dal with 1 bowl of any cooked vegetable

Before sleeping: ½ tsp raw unfiltered ACV in water

THE LIFESTYLE DIET PLAN NO. 90

(Smoothie detox diet)

Upon waking up: 1 tsp turmeric + ½ tsp ACV in lukewarm water + 1 capsule Vibact DS

20 min before breakfast: 1 cup black coffee with 1 tsp cold-pressed coconut oil

Breakfast: 1 glass morning smoothie made with fresh berries + avocado + banana + almond milk + pumpkin seeds + 1 tsp cinnamon powder + 1 scoop collagen powder + 2 ashwagandha tablets

Mid-morning snack: 1 bowl mixed seeds (pumpkin, sunflower, flax and chia) + 1 cup herbal tea (ginger, basil leaves, lemongrass, turmeric, green tea leaves) with lemon

Lunch: smoothie made with 5 almonds + 5 walnuts + ½ apple + ½ avocado + 1 slice of pineapple + 1 bowl baby spinach and parsley + coconut milk + 1 tsp cinnamon powder

Mid-evening juice: 1 glass celery juice with amla extract and 1 tsp sabza seeds

Dinner (3–4 hours before sleeping): smoothie with strawberries + 1 small banana + 5 hazelnuts + 5 pecans + ½ avocado + some almond milk as per the required consistency

THE LIFESTYLE DIET PLAN NO. 91

(Detox diet routine)

Upon waking up: 1 cup water (normal temp) with wheatgrass juice and lemon + 1 Vibact DS capsule

Before morning workout: 1 cup ghee coffee (black coffee with 1 tsp cow ghee)

Breakfast: lemon/ginger/tulsi tea + 1 bowl cooked sprouted matki with tomatoes, onions and lemon juice

Mid-morning snack: 1 glass juice (celery + carrots + cucumber + ½ inch ginger + lemon)

Lunch: steamed vegetables (cauliflower, broccoli, spinach, bell peppers) with sprouted chickpeas + homemade buttermilk (1 glass)

Mid-afternoon snack: 1 bowl freshly cut strawberries + 7 almonds + 4 walnut halves + 1 cup herbal tea (basil + turmeric + green tea leaves + lemongrass + cardamom + lemon)

Dinner: pumpkin/sweet potatoes/carrots and zucchini soup + sprouts sabzi (any; 1 bowl) with pickles + radish on the side

Before sleeping: 1 glass water with 1 tsp raw unfiltered ACV

THE LIFESTYLE DIET PLAN NO. 92

(Intermittent fasting diet plan)

9:00 a.m. (morning drink): 1 tsp turmeric + ½ tsp ACV in barley water or plain water

9:20 a.m.: 1 cup ghee coffee or coconut coffee

10:15 a.m. (breakfast): 1 moong dal chilla with pudina chutney

or

1 dosa or thepla with chutney

2:30 p.m. (lunch): 1 millet roti + 1 bowl of any green leafy vegetable + 1 bowl dal + raw salad or koshimbir on the side

Mid-evening snack: 1 bowl mixed seeds + 6 almonds + 1 cup green tea with lemon

or

1 glass carrot and cucumber juice + ½ lemon + sabza seeds

5:00 p.m. (dinner): 1 bowl homemade cauliflower/mushroom soup/tomato/red pumpkin/sweet potato soup + cooked sprouts (moong/matki/chavali/masoor) + 1 bowl raita (homemade)

THE LIFESTYLE DIET PLAN NO. 93

(Diet for pregnancy)

Upon waking up: 1 glass warm water with lemon and ghee and a pinch of haldi + a smoothie with mangoes or any seasonal fruit + 5 soaked almonds + 4 walnuts + 5 soaked resins + 1 fig + 2 dates + fresh coconut malai or avocado + water as per the required consistency

Breakfast: homemade methi paratha with chutney or dosa with coconut chutney or oats porridge with nuts and seeds

Lunch: moong chilla/ragi dosa or vegetable thepla with coconut chutney

or

2 eggs bhurji or omelette with chilla or ragi roti

or

1 ragi roti + 1 bowl of any green leafy vegetable + 1 bowl dal + 1 bowl raita or buttermilk

Evening snack: 1 glass milk with mixed seeds or coconut water with pumpkin seeds

Dinner: 1 bowl asparagus soup or sweet potato soup + 1 bowl soaked brown rice with mixed vegetable curry or dal or sprouts curry

Midnight snacking options: Dry fruits ladoo or roasted seeds or roasted makhana or peanut jaggery ladoo

THE LIFESTYLE DIET PLAN NO. 94

(Routine diet plan)

Morning drink: 1 glass barley water with 1 tsp raw unfiltered ACV and ½ tsp turmeric

Pre- or post-workout snack: 1 cup black coffee with 1 tbsp ghee or coconut oil

2:15 p.m. (lunch): 1 bowl cooked sprouts with tomatoes, onions, cucumber, a pinch of rock salt, black pepper and lemon juice

or

Homemade fish or chicken salad with red or black rice

4:00 p.m. (mid-evening snack): 1 bowl mixed seeds + 5 almonds + 5 walnuts + 1 fig

6:00 p.m. (dinner): 1 bowl quinoa rice + 1 bowl cooked vegetables (all seasonal) + 1 bowl dal + raw onion, tomato, radish and cucumber on the side

Before sleeping: 1 glass barley water

THE LIFESTYLE DIET PLAN NO. 95

(Routine diet plan)

Upon waking up: 1 glass barley water with 1 tsp raw unfiltered ACV and ½ tsp turmeric

Before workout: 1 cup black coffee with 1 tsp coconut oil

Morning workout and yoga

Breakfast: smoothie made with papaya + cucumber + green apple + spinach + ½ avocado or coconut malai + chia and sabza seeds

Mid-morning snack: 5 almonds + 5 walnuts + 1 dried fig + 1 cup herbal tea

Lunch: 1–2 ragi or moong chilla or millet roti with cooked vegetables (all seasonal) + 1 bowl dal + raw onion, tomato, radish and cucumber on the side

Evening snacks: 1 cup green tea with lemon or herbal tea + 1 bowl roasted mixed seeds (sunflower, pumpkin, flax, chia)

Dinner: tomato/cauliflower/red pumpkin soup + cooked kidney beans or chavali or matki or black chana salad (kidney beans + cherry tomatoes + bell peppers + broccoli); cook this well and add lemon juice on top

Before sleeping: ½ tsp raw unfiltered ACV in barley water

THE LIFESTYLE DIET PLAN NO. 96

(Detox diet plan)

Upon waking up: 1 cup water (normal temp) with wheatgrass powder and lemon

Breakfast: 1 cup butter coffee with 7 soaked almonds

Lunch: vegetables salad with mushrooms

or

moong dosa/chilla + homemade buttermilk (2 glasses)

Mid-afternoon snack: 1 bowl mixed seeds with 7 almonds + 4 walnuts + 1 Vibact DS capsule

Dinner: boiled vegetable soup + 1 bowl cooked chickpeas with pickles (homemade)

Before sleeping: 1 glass water with lemon or amla juice

Tip: You can eat nuts and seeds in case you are hungry between meals.

THE LIFESTYLE DIET PLAN NO. 97

(Detox diet plan)

9:00 a.m.: 1 glass normal water with 1 tbsp ACV

Breakfast: 1 glass morning smoothie made with green apple + banana + almond milk + pumpkin seeds + 1 tsp cinnamon powder

Lunch: 1 bowl cooked matki + moong sprouts with 1 bowl vegetables (cooked)

Mid-evening snack: 1 cup butter coffee with 1 bowl mixed seeds

Dinner (6:30 p.m.): smoothie made with carrots + cucumber + banana + coconut malai + water

Before sleeping: 1 tbsp ACV in normal water

THE LIFESTYLE DIET PLAN NO. 98

(Detox diet plan)

Breakfast: lemon/ginger/tulsi tea + 1 bowl quinoa upma or porridge

Mid-morning snack: juice made with pomegranate + carrots + pumpkin and sunflower seeds + almonds + radish

Lunch: green smoothie (with any three different-coloured veggies) + mixed dry fruits + 1 tsp coconut oil + dahi + water

Mid-afternoon snack: plain celery or kale juice with black pepper and pink salt/rock salt

Dinner: boiled vegetable salad with moong dal or tofu

THE LIFESTYLE DIET PLAN NO. 99

(Detox diet plan)

Upon waking up: 1 glass water with lemon and a pinch of turmeric + 1 Vibact DS capsule

Breakfast: Butter coffee (1tbsp ghee + 1 tbsp ghee/coconut oil) + 6–7 soaked almonds + 5 soaked walnuts

Mid-morning snack: 1 glass (pomegranate + radish) juice with 1 tsp sabza seeds

Lunch: boiled vegetable (with Italian herbs, pepper and sea salt) salad with cooked sprouted moong dal or with tofu

or

1 bowl guacamole with carrots and cucumber sticks

Mid-afternoon snack: 1 cup herbal tea (ajwain, green tea, saunf, jeera, haldi, ginger) with mixed seeds

Dinner: tofu or chickpeas frankie/roll with lots of vegetables in millet roti

Before sleeping: 1 glass water + 1 Vibact DS capsule + 2 Triphala tablets

THE LIFESTYLE DIET PLAN NO. 100

(Routine diet plan)

Upon waking up: 1 tsp turmeric + ½ tsp ACV in normal water

Breakfast: 1 cup black coffee (with 1 tsp ghee or coconut oil + 1 tsp haldi + 1 scoop collagen)

or

1 glass morning smoothie with 1 banana + 1 tbsp overnight soaked oats + 5 soaked almonds + 1 tbsp mixed seeds + 1 tsp raw cacao powder + coconut malai or almond milk

or

2 eggs bhurji

Mid-morning snack: 8 almonds + 5 walnuts + 1 cup green tea with lemon

Lunch: 1 ragi/jowar roti + 1 bowl dal + 1 bowl of any seasonal cooked vegetables or grilled fish or egg curry/bhurji + 1 bowl raita

Mid-evening snack: 1 bowl roasted makhana chivda + 1 cup herbal tea

Dinner (before 7:30 p.m.; 3–4 hours before sleeping): homemade dal khichadi with ghee and pickles on the side

THE LIFESTYLE DIET PLAN NO. 101

Upon waking up: 1 glass plain water with 1 tsp raw unfiltered ACV and 1 tsp turmeric

Yoga or workout for 60 min

15–20 min meditation

Breakfast: 1–2 dosas/uttapam + coconut chutney + 1 tsp cow ghee + 1 egg (boiled; with yolk)

Mid-morning snack: herbal tea with lemon and honey

Lunch: 1 bowl brown rice (soaked in water for at least 4 hours) + 1 bowl cooked vegetables + 1 bowl dal (yellow or black) + raw radish, tomato and onion

or

1 bowl brown rice and green Thai curry

After lunch: 1 glass buttermilk (using homemade dahi and rock salt)

Mid-evening snack: mixed dry fruits bowl (5 almonds + 5 walnuts + 5 cashews + 5 pistachios) + 1 cup black coffee

Evening walk for 60 min

Dinner: 1–2 moong chilla or thalipith or bhakri with vegetables (you can add any Indian masala if you like) and any homemade curry + homemade pickle/chutney on the side + raw radish, tomato and onions

Before sleeping: 1 cup green tea or digestive tea

21
The Lifestyle Diary

LET'S DO THIS TOGETHER!

WHEN YOU GET on the Lifestyle Diet, this is going to be your daily checklist.

Note: Please take a photocopy of page two (Daily Checklist) and make ninety copies for the first ninety days. Alternatively, you can download the checklist here: https://www.nutracylifestyle.com/product-details/The-Lifestyle-Diet-Diary

Page 1

1. Name:
2. Age:
3. Profession:
4. Health goal:

5. Date of starting the Lifestyle Diet:

6. Why did you start reading *The Lifestyle Diet*?

7. What are the changes that you want to see in yourself permanently?

8. List down your greatest blessings:

9. List ten good things about yourself:

Page 2

Daily Checklist

1. Did you have your morning drink of butter coffee or ghee with warm water today?

2. Did you do your morning workout today?

3. What are the five things that you are grateful for today?

4. What did you have for the following meals today?
   Breakfast:
   Lunch:
   Dinner:
   Snacks:

5. How much water did you drink today?

6. Did you say thank you to each meal before eating?

7. Did you go on a post-dinner walk (Shatapavali)?

8. What are the five good things that happened to you today?

9. What is your weight today?

10. What is your goal weight?

11. Did you walk for 45 minutes today?

12. How many litres of water did you drink today?

13. Did you practice deep breaths or meditate between your meetings today?

14. Did you appreciate yourself for the efforts you have been putting in for your self-growth?

15. Did you practice affirmations today?

16. Which is favourite healthy food?

17. Which is your peak craving period and what helps you deal with it positively?

18. Are you an emotional eater?

Page 3

Progress chart:

Goals accomplished after Week 1:
Goals accomplished after Week 2:
Goals accomplished after Week 4:
Goals accomplished after Week 6:
Goals accomplished after Week 8:
Goals accomplished after Week 10:
Goals accomplished after Week 12:
Goals accomplished after Week 14:
Goals accomplished after Week 16:
After sixteen weeks, write down ten things that have completely changed in your lifestyle forever.

1.
2.
3.
4.
5.
6.
7.
8.
9.
10.

Bibliography

ACS (2012), 'Strong Scientific Evidence That Eating Berries Benefits the Brain', 7 March, ACS News Service Weekly PressPac, https://www.acs.org/content/acs/en/pressroom/presspacs/2012/acs-presspac-march-7-2012/strong-scientific-evidence-that-eating-berries-benefits-the-brain.html

Allen, Summer (2018), 'Is Gratitude Good for Your Health?', https://greatergood.berkeley.edu/article/item/is_gratitude_good_for_your_health

Babauta, Leo (n.d.), 'Meditation for Beginners: 20 Practical Tips for Understanding the Mind', Zen Habits, https://zenhabits.net/meditation-guide/

BFC.Green (n.d.), 'A Guide to Salad Greens', http://bfc.green/blog/2017/02/28/a-guide-to-salad-greens/

Brown, George (n.d.) 'Breakfast Choices That Keep You from Losing Weight', WREG.com, https://wreg.com/news/breakfast-choices-that-keep-you-from-losing-weight/amp/

Cohen, Yaniv (2020), 'What Is Spirulina and It's Benefits', 23 August, https://www.thespicedetective.com/blog/what-is-spirulina-and-its-benefits

Consciousevolution.TV (2021), 'Zig Zag Zen: The Zen Perspective on Psychedelics', 15 April, https://www.consciousevolution.tv/mental-attitude/ in-praise-of-gratitude-harvard-health.php

DeLuca, Hector F. (2004), 'Overview of General Physiologic Features and Functions of Vitamin D', *American Journal of Clinical Nutrition*, 80(6): 1689S–1696S.

Dosha Food Co., https://doshafoodco.com/benifits-of-ghee/

Dr Denese, https://drdenese.com/blogs/news/collagen-benefits-for-skin-joints-gut-and-more

Dr Farrah MD, https://www.drfarrahmd.com/2020/05/the-skin-benefits-of-vitamin-c.html

Freeman, W.H. (2000), 'Collagen: The Fibrous Proteins of the Matrix' (Section 22.3), in H. Lodish, A. Berk, S.L. Zipursky, et al. (eds), *Molecular Cell Biology* (4th edition). New York, https://www.ncbi.nlm.nih.gov/books/NBK21582/

Freire, Thiago (2017), 'Anti-aging Detox: You Are What You Eat', Wellness, 18 December, https://wsimag.com/wellness/33963-anti-aging-detox

Food Pharmacy Blog, https://foodpharmacy.blog/now-foods-brazil-nuts-organic.html

García-Figueiras, Roberto, Sandra Baleato-González, Anwar R. Padhani, et al. (2019), 'How Clinical Imaging Can Assess Cancer Biology', *Insights Imaging*, doi: 10.1186/s13244-019-0703-0

Gebhardt, Susan E. and Robin G. Thomas (2002), 'Nutritive Value of Foods', U.S. Department of Agriculture, Agricultural Research Service, *Home and Garden Bulletin*, 72.

Harvard Health Publishing, https://www.health.harvard.edu/mind-and-mood/in-praise-of-gratitude

Healing Naturally, 'Leaky Gut Syndrome', https://www.sallypattison.com.au/leaky-gut-syndrome/

Healthline, https://www.healthline.com/nutrition/8-benefits-of-nuts

Healthline (n.d.), 'What Is Barley Grass? Everything You Need to Know', https://www.healthline.com/nutrition/barley-grass

International Yoga Association (2017), 'Types of Pranayama', 14 August, https://internationalyogaassociation.wordpress.com/

Jenkinson, Howard F. and L. Julia Douglas. (2002), 'Interactions between Candida Species and Bacteria in Mixed Infections', *Polymicrobial Diseases*, https://www.ncbi.nlm.nih.gov/books/NBK2486/

Jom Organics, https://www.jomorganics.com/post/the-top-10-health-benefits-of-turmeric-the-sacred-root-that-rejuvenates-the-body-and-mind

Liftique, https://liftique.com/benefits-of-an-epsom-salt-detox/

Lochab, Bimlesh, Swapnil Shuklaa and Indra K. Varmab (2014), 'Naturally Occurring Phenolic Sources: Monomers and Polymers', *RSC Advances*, 42.

Lunsford, Weston (2020), 'The Science of Gratitude', 18 August, Dental Intellegence, https://blog.dentalintel.com/posts/the-science-of-gratitude

Mahoney, Kelli (n.d.), 'A Simple Prayer of Gratitude', https://www.roundhillcommunitychurch.org/youth-1

Medical News Today (n.d.), 'What Are the Benefits of an Epson Salt Detox?', https://www.medicalnewstoday.com/articles/321627

Moghaddam, S.J., Barta, P., Mirabolfathinejad, S.G., et al. (2009), 'Curcumin inhibits COPD-like airway inflammation and lung cancer progression in mice', *Carcinogenesis* 30(11): 1949–56, doi: 10.1093/carcin/bgp229

MSM Guide (n.d.), 'Anti-aging/Skin', https://msmguide.com/beauty-from-within/

Mumme, Karen and Welma Stonehouse (2015), 'Effects of Medium-Chain Triglycerides on Weight Loss and Body Composition: A Meta-analysis of Randomized Controlled Trials', *Journal of the Academy of Nutrition and Dietetics*, doi: 10.1016/j.jand.2014.10.022

Muskoka C.B.D., https://www.muskokacbd.com/raw-unrefined-coconut-oil-cold-pres

Natgene, https://www.natgene.net/microbiota-en

Norton Healthcare, https://nortonhealthcare.com/news/5-power-foods-for-better-urinary-health/

Ogbolu, David Olusoga, Anthony Alaba Oni and Oluwole Adebayo Daini (2007), 'In Vitro Antimicrobial Properties of Coconut Oil on Candida Species in Ibadan, Nigeria', *Journal of Medicine Food*, doi: 10.1089/jmf.2006.1209

Perfect Juicing, https://perfectjuicing.com/the-best-green-smoothie-recipe-ever/

Koníčková, Renata, Kateřina Vaňková, Jana Vaníková, et al. (2014). 'Anti-cancer Effects of Blue-Green Alga Spirulina Platensis, a Natural Source of Bilirubin-Like Tetrapyrrolic Compounds', *Annals of Hepatology*, 13(2): 273–83.

Sengupta, Sushmita (2018), 'Neem for Diabetes: How Does the Wonder Herb Help Manage Blood Sugar Levels', NDTV Food, 6 August, https://food.ndtv.com/food-drinks/neem-for-diabetes-how-does-the-wonder-herb-help-manage-blood-sugar-levels-1895965

Shmerling, Robert H. (2020), 'Apple cider vinegar diet: Does it really work?', 29 October, *Harvard Health Blog*, https://www.health.harvard.edu/blog/apple-cider-vinegar-diet-does-it-really-work-2018042513703

Siddiqui, Fahad Javaid, Pryseley Nkouibert Assam, Nurun Nisa de Souza, et al. (2018), 'Diabetes Control: Is Vinegar a Promising Candidate to Help Achieve Targets?',

Journal of Evidence-Based Integrative Medicine, doi: 10.1177/2156587217753004

Sivamaruthi, Bhagavathi Sundaram, Periyanaina Kesika and Chaiyavat Chaiyasut (2018), 'A Review on Anti-aging Properties of Probiotics', *International Journal of Applied Pharmaceutics*, September, doi: 10.22159/ijap.2018v10i5.28249

slmtnoush.com https://slmtnoush.com/shop/mixed-berry-infusion/?lang=en

Smartness Health, https://www.smartnesshealth.com/health/essential-for-the-body/

Tandy, Patrick (2018) 'Midyear Meeting and State of Profession', *Bar Bulletin*, 15 March, https://ampupfitness.com/wp-content/uploads/2017/10/HealthWellnessMarch2018.pdf

Tiwari, Ruchi, Amit Kumar Verma, Sandip Chakraborty et al. (2014), 'Neem (Azadirachta indica) and its Potential for Safeguarding Health of Animals and Humans: A Review', *Journal of Biological Sciences*, 14: 110–123.

Uruakpa, Florence O., M.A.H Ismond and E.N.T Akobundu (2002), 'Colostrum and Its Benefits: A Review', *Nutrition Research*, 22(6): 755–767, doi: 10.1016/S0271-5317(02)00373-1

Vieira, Ginger (2019), 'Nuts and Diabetes: Are Nuts a Good Snack for People with Diabetes?', https://diabetesstrong.com/nuts-diabetes/

Woman's World, https://www.womansworld.com/posts/aging/vitamin-d-benefits-132890

Woman's World, https://www.womansworld.com/posts/aging/zinc-for-hair-and-skin-173893

World Health Organization (WHO), (2018), 'Arsenic', 15 February, https://www.who.int/news-room/fact-sheets/detail/arsenic

World Health Organization (2021), 'Diabetes', https://www.who.int/news-room/fact-sheets/detail/diabetes

Yoga Point India (n.d.), 'Pranayama: From Hatha Yoga to Ashtanga Yoga', https://www.yogapoint.com/pranayama/types-of-pranayama.htm

Zuma Nutrition, https://www.zumanutrition.com/blogs/health/ pau-darco-featured-in-our-liver-detox-formula

About the Author

Dr Rohini Patil, MBBS, is a passionate nutritionist and founder of Nutracy Lifestyle. She has successfully written and implemented over 1,200 diet plans for her clients. An official nutritionist on board with National Indian Athletes (GAIL, NYCS), Patil has won awards such as the FSSAI Eat Right Award (as social media influencer). Patil has been a guest lecturer of diet and nutrition at various institutions and health events. She has also participated in the radio show called Healthy Lifestyle with Dr Rohini (since 2019) on Radio 94.3 Tomato broadcasted in Kolhapur, Maharashtra.

All content found within this book (including text, images, or any other formats), has been created for informational purposes only. The Content is not intended to be a substitute for professional medical advice, diagnosis, or treatment, and does not constitute medical advice. Always seek the advice of your physician or other qualified health provider with any questions you may have regarding a medical condition. Never disregard professional medical advice from your physician, or delay in seeking it for any conditions which you may have.